SHOULD I SHORT SALE
MY HOME?

Homeowners Guide: How To Survive The Worst Real Estate Market in History. In Today's Market A Smart Sale Is a Short Sale

by Christopher J Crippen

Co-Author's

Tim & Julie Harris

Disclaimer

Please note that the contents of this book are meant for reference only. The authors and co-authors are not accountants or attorneys. Individual housing and financial situations vary so seek the advice of a professional real estate agent, accountant and attorney to assess your specific situation and review your options. Bank laws and guidelines change on a daily basis so the reader is advised to speak directly with their lender to understand bank specific policies.

Table Of Contents

Chapter One

The Foreclosure Epidemic is Here… Are Your Ready?

Are you stressed out about mortgage payments? Do you think your only option is a foreclosure? Are you considering 'walking away'? Struggling with a loan modification? Is a short sale right for you? Millions and millions of homeowners are asking themselves the same questions. It is projected that over 20,000,000 homeowners will have negative equity in their homes by this time next year. In other words they will owe more on their homes than they are worth. Over 2.9 million homes have foreclosed in the last three years and the number is only expected to grow. Expect the effect of the real estate recession to ripple for years to come.

What can you do now?

There is expected to be a massive tsunami of homeowners who are simply making the decision to sell their homes through a short sale vs. staying in a home, hoping that one day it may be worth what they paid.

No one is safe. News stories from across the country tell the tales of both celebrities and the average American who are all considering selling their homes through a short sale.

Selling your home through a short sale need not be a shameful, life-ruining experience. Sometimes short selling your mortgage simply makes smart economic sense, especially for homeowners who find themselves "upside down" — that is, they owe more on their mortgage than their house is worth.

Late last year CNBC Financial Guru Jim Cramer was telling homeowners to 'Just Walk Away'. Watch the video on YouTube.com.

We are clearly in uncharted waters. The current housing crisis is different from all the previous housing recessions. It is now public knowledge that many financial institutions sold mortgages in a deceptive manner — for example, by approving people for loans they couldn't really afford — then why should homeowners feel obliged to honor their commitments? Skeptics argue there's a 'moral hazard'.

From the homeowner's perspective, why should they remain in homes that are depreciating? Often times it's possible to rent the same style home in the same area for half (or less) than their current mortgage payment. Assuming it takes years for the market to recover, the homeowner who sells their home via a short sale now will be further ahead financially than the person who 'stuck it out'.

Here is an example:

Starting May of 2010.

- Homeowner paid $500,000 at the market peak in late 2006. Homeowner put down 5% and did a 7-year interest only mortgage. Monthly payment including PITA and upkeep is $4200.

Property has depreciated 40% and is now worth only $300,000. Owner has negative equity or is 'upside down' by $200,000.

Market is continuing to depreciate and is projected to possibly level off in mid to late 2012. In other words, months and months of more losses for the homeowner. Many economists are predicting prices may NEVER recover to boom-level pricing.

Option 1

Our homeowner can 'stick it out' and keep the home. They will continue to make their monthly interest only payment/ house upkeep of $4200 per month. They will pay $50,400 per year to keep the home. They are deeply 'upside down' in the home with massive negative equity. Somewhere in late 2011 to mid 2012 the home's value has stopped depreciating. The market stays flat for at least a year thereafter, likely much longer. The inventory levels have to sell off. In late 2012 or early 2013 the market then starts to slowly appreciate again. Best case, the home starts to appreciate at 5% per year. Based on this rough example it will take at least 10 years for that home to be worth what that owner paid in 2006. During that time the homeowner will have paid $50,400 per year. Do the math. That's $352,000 spent to stay in the home to 'stick it out'. That's IF there's 5% appreciation and IF that's consistent for 10 years.

Option 2

Homeowner lists the home with an agent trained in doing short sales. The home sells and the bank agrees to accept the loss in equity as the short sale. Bank loses $200,000. Homeowner moves to a rental home in the same neighborhood and pays rent of $2000 per month or less…That's half of his previous house payment. Our homeowner no longer has to worry about repairs or property taxes while getting back on their feet. Our homeowner saves the difference between what he had been paying for the owned home and his new rent payment. **That's $26,400 per year**. Yes, the homeowner does have significant negative credit ramifications as a result of their short sale. This negative credit will prevent them from buying a home for the next 18-24 months. With this option he can sit out the real estate recession and jump back in when the market has hit bottom. If he times it right he can buy at the bottom of the market and have a significant down payment, resulting from the savings the created by downsizing their house payment. Some homeowners even experience faster credit recovery due to a more favorable debt-to-income ratio, by no longer having a big mortgage. Remember that your payment history accounts for 35% of your credit score; it is not your entire score. 30% is your length of credit history, 15% has to do with new credit established, 10% is the type of credit used, etc.

- http://articles.moneycentral.msn.com/Banking/your-credit-score.aspx

- www.EquiFax.com

- www.TransUnion.com

- www.Experian.com

Yes, there is damage to your credit

According to national experts, a person's credit will go down by 200 + or - points and then prevent them from buying using a government backed mortgage for up to 24 months. With a foreclosure, credit is damaged for up to 7 years, preventing someone from obtaining a government backed mortgage, and possibly any mortgage for a longer stretch. It's not just the ability to buy a home that is affected. Remember, even mobile phone companies check credit before assigning an account or having you sign a contract. An individual may pay more for insurance with a bigger credit ding from a foreclosure.

Many home owners who are now short selling their properties are going to want to buy houses again someday; and when they do, lenders are going to want to make money lending them money to do so. It's a matter of deciding how and when to exit a potentially toxic loan as gracefully as possible.

Chapter Two

How Bad Is It?

One thing that is certain: Foreclosures are on the rise. Cities in California, Ohio, Florida and Michigan posted the highest foreclosure rates in the U.S., according to RealtyTrac, a private firm known for accuracy of foreclosure data.

This information is from a recent report that they released. If you want to obtain current, up to the minute information on foreclosures in your area go to their website. www.realtytrac.com. You can type your city or zip code and find local data there.

RealtyTrac® (www.realtytrac.com), the leading online marketplace for foreclosure properties, today released its U.S. Foreclosure Market Report™ for Q3 2009, which shows that foreclosure filings — default notices, scheduled auctions and bank repossessions — were reported on 937,840 properties in the third quarter, a 5 percent increase from the previous quarter and an increase of nearly 23 percent from Q3 2008. One in every 136 U.S. housing units received a foreclosure filing during the quarter — the highest quarterly foreclosure rate since RealtyTrac began issuing its report in the first quarter of 2005.

Foreclosure filings were reported on 343,638 properties in September, a 4 percent decrease from the previous month but a 29 percent increase from September 2008. Despite the monthly decrease, September's total was still the third highest monthly total since the RealtyTrac report began in January 2005, behind only July and August of this year.

"Bank repossessions, or REOs, jumped 21 percent from the second quarter to the third quarter, corresponding to jumps in defaults and scheduled auctions in the previous two quarters," said James J. Saccacio, chief executive officer of RealtyTrac. "REO activity increased from the previous quarter in all but two states and the District of Columbia, indicating that lenders may be starting to work through some of the pent-up foreclosure inventory caused by legislative delays, loan modification efforts and high volumes of distressed properties."

Report methodology *The RealtyTrac U.S. Foreclosure Market Report provides a count of the total number of properties with at least one foreclosure filing reported during the month or quarter — broken out by type of filing at the state and national level. Data is also available at the individual county level for both Q1 2009 and March 2009. Data is collected from more than 2,200 counties nationwide, and those counties account for more than 90 percent of the U.S. population. RealtyTrac's report incorporates documents filed in all three phases of foreclosure: Default — Notice of Default (NOD) and Lis Pendens (LIS); Auction — Notice of Trustee Sale and Notice of Foreclosure Sale (NTS and NFS); and Real Estate Owned, or REO properties (that have been foreclosed on and repurchased by a bank). If more than one foreclosure document is filed against a property during the month or quarter, only the most recent filing is counted in the report.*

Additionally, use the RealtyTrac resources to find out what's happening in your own back yard:

IRVINE, Calif. – Oct. 7, 2010 *– RealtyTrac® (www.realtytrac.com), the leading online marketplace for foreclosure properties, today announced the release of an exclusive recently sold feature that allows users to see detailed information for all properties that sold in the last three, six and nine months in any given area.*

"The new recently sold feature will help our users determine what buyers have recently paid for properties in any neighborhood nationwide," said James J. Saccacio, chief executive officer of RealtyTrac. "That knowledge is extremely useful for many different types of users for different reasons. It will help homebuyers determine how much to offer; it will help sellers determine how much to ask; it will help homeowners determine how much their property is worth; and it will help investors determine the profit and cash flow potential of a neighborhood."

RealtyTrac is the only real estate website that combines recently sold data with foreclosure properties and Multiple Listing Service (MLS) information. RealtyTrac users can search 2.5 million recently sold properties. Subscribers also have access to more than 2 million properties in some stage of foreclosure, and can also view another 1.5 MLS listings for sale. Collectively, these three data sets — recently sold listings, foreclosure properties and MLS listings — account for 6 million properties.

Subscribers will be able to view property details — including the number of bedrooms, bathrooms, square footage, lot size, and year built — for recently sold properties. In addition, they will see the sales price, sales date, and the foreclosure status of the property when it sold. The recently sold data includes both properties in foreclosure and properties not in foreclosure.

An interactive map plots the location of recently sold properties in relation to other properties posted on RealtyTrac, giving users the ability to compare recently sold properties to nearby pre-foreclosures, auctions, bank-owned homes, and resale homes. Subscription is required for full access to the new recently sold feature.

(Rather than paying for a subscription for this data, ask your local Real Estate professional who specializes in short sales and foreclosures. They will have access to that information and provide it to you for free with a confidential consultation. If you don't know who that is in your area, call us for a free referral 866 422 9497).

Chapter Three

Ok, I Get It…A Short Sale May Be My Best Option…Tell Me More…

A short sale is when a lender accepts a discount on a mortgage to avoid a possible foreclosure auction or bankruptcy. For example: A homeowner, who is facing foreclosure, has an existing first mortgage of $500,000. The market value of the home is $350,000.

Long story short, the lender accepts the offer for $350,000 and the home is sold.

That's a short sale.

Why are lenders so eager to take such a huge discount? Banks do not like bad loans. If they see an opportunity where they can sell the property without the huge loss of a foreclosure, they will do it. Some lenders report that if the home goes into foreclosure by the time the home actually closes with the new buyer the lender will be lucky to have netted 50% of the original loan balance.

What's the bottom line from the lenders perspective? They are in the business of lending money, not owning homes. If they can accept a short sale offer and rid themselves of the bad loan AND net more vs. the home going into foreclosure...they will do it every time. It's simply smart business for them. This is even more valid now that the writing is on the wall. The foreclosure crisis has reached epidemic proportions. Every day there's a new report about the sheer numbers of 'shadow inventory', or homes that have been foreclosed on but haven't gotten back on the market yet. There are millions of homes already in the shadow inventory pipeline. Banks are not anxious to increase those numbers any more.

Time is not on your side when you are considering a short sale. You must act quickly and work only with a real estate expert who has successfully completed and graduated from advanced real estate education programs like Harris Real Estate University. Not every real estate professional is trained in this type of transaction. A highly skilled professional can take the weight off your shoulders and help you to make a decision that's right for your family and your situation.

I heard short sales are hard to close!

Up until now, the real estate market, including Realtors, Lenders, Servicers, title companies, etc, have been sorting out how to do short sales in an efficient way. It's no surprise that this has taken some time to figure out.

Fortunately, things are improving. The Home Affordable Foreclosure Alternatives, or HAFA program, aims to streamline the process.

HAFA establishes streamlined short sale rules and incentivizes borrowers and lenders to work together to avoid foreclosure. The rules -- in effect between April 5, 2010, and Dec. 31, 2012 -- also are intended to speed up the short sale process.

"The streamlined short sales process will definitely help homeowners," says David Liniger, Re/Max International chairman and co-founder.

Eligibility requirements

The HAFA guidelines apply to lenders who voluntarily participate in the HAMP (Home Affordable Modification Program). The Department of

Housing and Urban Development says more than 100 servicers have signed up to participate in HAMP, covering more than 89 percent of mortgage debt outstanding in the country.

Find out more about your loan using the Loan Look-Up Tool here:

http://makinghomeaffordable.gov/loan_lookup.html

To be eligible for HAFA, homeowners must first apply for a loan modification through the Home Affordable Modification Program, or HAMP. *Homeowners who do not qualify for a loan modification or miss payments during the initial loan modification period qualify for HAFA.*

Other HAFA requirements include:

- Property is homeowner's principal residence.

- The Mortgage was originated before Jan. 1, 2009.

- Mortgage is owned or guaranteed by Fannie Mae or Freddie Mac.

- Borrower is delinquent or default is foreseeable.

- Homeowner demonstrates hardship.

- Borrower's total monthly housing payment exceeds 31 percent of gross income.

- Unpaid principal does not exceed $729,750.

According to HAFA rules, lenders now must offer a short sale in writing to the borrower within 30 days if the borrower does not qualify for or complete a loan modification. Borrowers then must respond within 14 days to the lender's short sale agreement.

Chapter Four

What is Mortgage Foreclosure?

Mortgage foreclosure simply means the deed can only be foreclosed through court action. Mortgage foreclosure is usually referred to as a judicial foreclosure.

A mortgage is a security document that allows the borrower to keep title of the property while using the property as security or collateral for a loan. The lender then places a lien on the property in the event the owner does not pay the agreed payment. When the borrower pays off the loan, the lender gives the borrower a satisfaction of mortgage that removes the lien from the property. About half the states in the U.S. use mortgage foreclosure as the means of satisfying the loan balance.

As with most mortgage foreclosure lawsuits, it starts with a summons and a complaint is issued to the borrower and any other parties with inferior rights in the property. Usually the lenders attorney is the one who issues the notice. The complaint is usually filed in the court where the trial is to be held. Here is the interesting part. Once the borrower has been notified, he or she has 20 days to respond back to the court challenging them on the mortgage foreclosure lawsuit. Once this occurs, the court typically has 40 days to respond back to the borrower. Keep in mind that each correspondence must be legitimate and deal with some specific part of the complaint. This process may go back and forth as long as the borrower finds something erroneous with the complaint. This slows a mortgage foreclosure greatly because it must go through the court system. It may go as long as a year if necessary or even longer. This is how many homeowners stay in their homes for months often years after they have stopped making their house payments.

Most homeowners eventually decide to short sale the home, a) to avoid foreclosure and b) because even if they extend and pursue a foreclosure lawsuit, ultimately they will have to move, and the short sale many times costs nothing to the homeowner.

Chapter Five

You Have Been Warned. Foreclosure Scams on the Rise!

Foreclosure Scams are on the rise because of the increasing number of foreclosures. It's very important as homeowners to know about these scams.

Common Foreclosure Scams

1. Equity Skimming:

A "buyer" who offers to buy your home at full asking price approaches you. The potential buyer claims he will solve all your financial problems by "promising" to pay off your mortgage. He claims to take over the existing mortgage and give you a sum of money after the property is sold. But in order to do so, he suggests that you move out right away and deed the property over to him. So you move out and assume the "buyer" will continue to make the mortgage payments. However, the "buyer" collects rent for the next 6 - 8 months and does not make any mortgage payments. The lender has no choice but to foreclose and all the while you have no idea what's happening because you've moved out.

2. The Bait-And-Switch:

Very similar to taking over "subject to", but the acclaimed buyer is only after the equity. The buyer tells the homeowners he will bring the mortgage current and tells them they can stay in the home. But in order to do so, he must have a few documents signed that protect his interest and gives him ownership of the property. Then a few weeks down the road, the homeowner receives an eviction notice.

3. The Bailout:

Again very similar to the previous two, where the homeowners sign over the deed with the assumption that they will be able to remain in the house as a renter or lease it back from the buyer and eventually buy it back over time. The terms of these types of scams are so harsh that they make it nearly impossible to buy-back, which was the plan to begin with. The homeowner is left with nothing and the buyer walks off with most or all of the equity.

4. Phantom Assistance:

Typically these are online companies claiming to have the magic touch in stopping the foreclosure auction. They know all the ins and outs and what to say to the lender to stop the auction. Then these companies charge outrageous fees for simple phone calls and paperwork the homeowner could have done themselves.

5. Counseling Agencies:

Some groups, most of them online, calling themselves "counseling agencies" may approach you or ask you to submit your information for a personal consultation to review your situation. They then proceed to offer certain services for a fee. Most of the time these "special services" you are paying for are FREE, such as negotiating a new payment plan with your lender, working out a forbearance, or lowering your interest rate. These are all things your lender will assist you with at no charge. Be careful giving ANYONE money online that claims they can assist you out of foreclosure. There are dozens of good, non-profit organizations and free counseling agencies that are ready and willing to assist.

6. Short Sale Companies:

This is the newest breed of companies to avoid. Here is the bottom line; they make all their money from the fees you pay them at the start of the process. In other words, they have little to no incentive to get your short sale actually accepted and closed.

One of the largest foreclosure assistance programs right now is 888-995-HOPE. This is available to any homeowner in America having trouble paying their mortgage. It is provided free of charge by the Homeownership Preservation Foundation, a nonprofit dedicated to preserving homeownership.

Here are a few things you can do to avoid scams:

- **DON'T SIGN** any papers that you don't fully understand, or you could make bad matters worse.

- **DON'T SIGN** any papers that you feel pressured into signing. Take your time.

- **DON'T MAKE** mortgage payments to anyone other than your lender.

- **DON'T SIGN** over the deed without some closure or agreement for your protection. Talk to your attorney or title company if you need help.

- **DON'T EVER** pay anyone who claims to stop foreclosure. You can stop the auction yourself.

Chapter Six

What are the Options For Homeowners in Foreclosure?

1. Try to "make nice" with your lender.

You can call your lender and ask them to reinstate the loan. You may be allowed to reinstate or make the loan current by paying a lump sum or making scheduled payments to your lender over a given amount of time. Just explain to them you had a few bad months and things are now better and most lenders will try to work something out with you. If you call the number on your mortgage payment ticket or your bill, you'll be talking to the 'servicing' department. Their job is to take your money. You may need to speak with a supervisor or be transferred to their 'loss mitigation' or 'retention' department.

2. If you have equity, and have not missed payments, refinance.

Usually the lender would refinance the existing loan and include as part of the new loan any late payments, and fees that you would need to regain control. It would all be "wrapped" into one mortgage. An appraisal will be ordered and a new application is usually required.

3. Assuming you have no equity and have to sell, you can list your home with a Realtor who has been trained how to do short sales.

In most cases, this is your best option to achieve a graceful exit from the situation. It is almost always the least expensive to you and the least damaging to your credit. Remember: your lender pays all commissions and fees...listing with a short sale specialist costs you $0.00!

4. You can give the property back to the lender.

If there are no other liens on the title, the lender may agree to take the property back. This process of transferring ownership from you to the lender under these circumstances is called a Deed in Lieu of Foreclosure, and is sometimes referred to as a "friendly foreclosure" because in essence that what it is. You just walk away. Now that there are so many foreclosures already in the pipeline, lenders are tightening their requirements for a Deed in Lieu. Your home must be on the market for 90 days in many cases and you must have at least attempted a short sale. Call your lender and ask what they require, or contact your real estate professional and they can inquire on your behalf. Remember, a Deed In Lieu is STILL a foreclosure, in spite of the name.

5. You can file bankruptcy.

First, you need to seek the advice of an attorney. In no way are we trying to provide legal advice. Only an attorney can give legal advice. The two most common "chapters" of bankruptcy are Chapter 7 and Chapter 13.

Bankruptcies are either "work out" or "wipe out". Chapter 7 is the "wipe out" and Chapter 13 is the "work out". Bankruptcy is a federal court action designed to help individuals repay their debts or eliminate their debts depending on their circumstances. Chapter 13 bankruptcies are designed to reorganize debts in an effort to repay all debt. Chapter 7 bankruptcies are geared more towards liquidation of assets. Both Chapter 7 and Chapter 13 immediately stop the foreclosure process and any creditors from taking further action against you.

6. You can try to get a Loan Modification.

What is a loan modification? A loan modification occurs you're your mortgage lender restructures your mortgage in order to lower your payment to a manageable amount. Typically lowering the interest rate, extending the term of the loan, and possibly reducing the principle amount owed achieve the modification. Usually a combination of lower rate and longer term achieves a temporarily lower payment. Sometimes loan modification changes can be permanent for the life of the loan. A small amount of loan modifications include a principle reduction, but this is rare. The typical loan modification lowers the interest rate for a finite amount of time, such as 2% for 3 years, and then adjusts to market rates.

Loan modifications are also known as a loan restructure, a work out plan, or a mortgage modification.

The borrower, or homeowner, must be facing a verifiable, document able hardship. A hardship letter of explanation is required, along with financial statements showing that the situation has changed since the loan was written.

The goal of a workout plan or loan modification is to make the mortgage affordable and sustainable for the homeowner, and to turn a non-performing loan into a performing loan for the lender. The target is for the payment to be 31% or less of the homeowner's gross monthly income.

For information on the Home Affordable Modification Program, or HAMP and to see if you qualify, follow this link: http://makinghomeaffordable.gov/modification_eligibility.html. If you are not currently employed, do not have verifiable income, or a verifiable hardship, it is unlikely for you to be successful in the pursuit of a loan modification. If you are unsure of what to do next, contact your real estate professional. Your trusted real estate advisor, who has been trained in short sales, will also be able to help you determine if you should pursue a loan modification or not.

Who is eligible for a loan modification?

According to the Department of Treasury: "Anyone with high combined mortgage debt compared to income or who is "underwater" (with a combined mortgage balance higher than the current market value of his house) may be eligible for a loan modification. This initiative will also include borrowers who show other indications of being at risk of default. Eligibility for the program will sunset at the end of three years."

Who is NOT eligible for a loan modification? Speculators or those who bought homes for investment purposes. There are limited examples of loan modifications on rental or investment property. Loan modifications are considered on a case-by-case basis, but generally lenders who believe the owner is or was a 'flipper' or 'investor', have a much harder time getting a loan modification approved.

To help you sort out what to do as a homeowner considering loan modification or short sale, ask yourself these questions:

- Do I want to keep the house? (If yes, a loan modification could be a good solution for you…if no, a short sale is the better choice, assuming you owe more than the home is worth).

- Do I have a verifiable and document able income? (This is required for a loan modification, as it is a fully documented loan. If you cannot verify and document income, your loan mod will not be approvable).

- Can I afford a payment of 31% of my gross monthly income? (Some homeowners have so much consumer or other debt load that the home loan isn't the problem, it's everything else).

- What if I get a loan mod but the payment isn't much better, and I still have negative equity? What will I do with the home then? What's my back up plan?

- If I knew I could sell this home without having to cover the Real Estate commissions and closing costs, and have a professional agent negotiate on my behalf with my lender, would I want to keep it or sell it?

- What's best for my family? What's the next step?

- What happens if I do nothing?

- How long can I wait before it's too late?

Chapter 7

When someone files a Chapter 7 bankruptcy, all assets are frozen. The attorney creates what is called an automatic stay. Meaning everything "Stays" put. The homeowners can't buy anything, they can't sell anything, and they can't even give away anything. If they try to sell their home, they couldn't. If they try to give away money in savings, they can't. Any unsecured debt like credit cards, unsecured loans, etc. are eliminated or wiped out. They do not exist anymore. Then the trustee or attorney who represents the court and the creditors will look at all the assets (house, car, furniture, equipment) anything of value and decide what must be liquidated to pay some of the debt that was wiped out.

If the homeowners are in the middle of foreclosure, a Chapter 7 will stop the foreclosure process. Usually banks will then ask the trustee to release the property from the automatic stay so they may continue with the foreclosure process. Once the property has been released from the bankruptcy, the foreclosure process starts right where it left off. Typically you have anywhere from 3-5 weeks until the foreclosure process begins again.

Chapter 13

When someone files a Chapter 13, they don't take all the assets and sell them. Instead they take all the monthly payments and discount them for pennies on the dollar. It's like a debt consolidation plan. Whatever amount is agreed upon has to be paid to the bankruptcy count every month for the next 3-5 years. So the homeowners get to keep their house, their cars, and all their assets. Now, as long as the homeowner stays current with the mortgage payments and pays the amount agreed upon, they will be fine. However, if any payments are missed, the trustee will dismiss the bankruptcy and the foreclosure process will begin again.

And finally, you can just let it go to foreclosure. Basically you don't do anything. You leave with nothing in hand and a foreclosure on your credit report. This is without question the worst option of all.

Another solution available is the **Soldier Relief Act of 1940**. When a property is owned by a person who is in the military and the mortgage payments are not made, then this relief act may stop foreclosure based on certain criteria. The person has to be in active duty in order to qualify. The mortgage loan had to be established before the soldier was called out to active duty. Not only will this stop foreclosure, but also it will stop seizure of any personal property while the soldier is actively serving and several months thereafter.

What is the Mortgage Forgiveness Debt Relief Act of 2007?

The Mortgage Forgiveness Debt Relief Act of 2007 was enacted on December 20, 2007 (http://www.irs.treas.gov/irs/article/0,,id=179073,00.html) see News Release IR-2008-17). Generally, the Act allows exclusion of income realized as a result of modification of the terms of the mortgage, or foreclosure on your principal residence.

What does that mean?

Usually, debt that is forgiven or cancelled by a lender must be included as income on your tax return and is taxable. The Mortgage Forgiveness Debt Relief Act of 2007 allows you to exclude certain cancelled debt on your principal residence from income.

Does the Mortgage Forgiveness Debt Relief Act of 2007 apply to all forgiven or cancelled debts?

No, the Act applies only to forgiven or cancelled debt used to buy, build or substantially improve your principal residence, or to refinance debt incurred for those purposes.

What about refinanced homes?

Debt used to refinance your home qualifies for this exclusion, but only up to the extent that the principal balance of the old mortgage, immediately before the refinancing, would have qualified.

Does this provision apply for the 2007 tax year only?

It applies to qualified debt forgiven in 2007, 2008 or 2009. If the forgiven debt is excluded from income, do I have to report it on my tax return?

Yes. The amount of debt forgiven must be reported on Form 982 and the Form 982 must be attached to your tax return.

Do I have to complete the entire Form 982?

(http://www.irs.treas.gov/pub/irs-pdf/f982.pdf) Form 982, Reduction of Tax Attributes Due to Discharge of Indebtedness (and Section 1082 Adjustment), is used for other purposes in addition to reporting the exclusion of forgiveness of qualified principal residence indebtedness. If you are using the form only to report the exclusion of forgiveness of qualified principal residence indebtedness as the result of foreclosure on your principal residence, you only need to complete lines 1e and 2. If you kept ownership of your home and modification of the terms of your mortgage resulted in the forgiveness of qualified principal residence indebtedness, complete lines 1e, 2, and 10b. Attach the Form 982 to your tax return.

Where can I get this form?

You can download the form at IRS.gov.

What is the Mortgage Forgiveness Debt Relief Act of 2007?

The Mortgage Forgiveness Debt Relief Act of 2007 was enacted on December 20, 2007 "http://www.irs.treas.gov/irs/article/0,,id=179073,00.html" see News Release IR-2008-17). Generally, the Act allows exclusion of income realized as a result of modification of the terms of the mortgage, or foreclosure on your principal residence.

What does that mean?

Usually, debt that is forgiven or cancelled by a lender must be included as income on your tax return and is taxable. The Mortgage Forgiveness Debt Relief Act of 2007 allows you to exclude certain cancelled debt on your principal residence from income.

Does the Mortgage Forgiveness Debt Relief Act of 2007 apply to all forgiven or cancelled debts?

No, the Act applies only to forgiven or cancelled debt used to buy, build or substantially improve your principal residence, or to refinance debt incurred for those purposes.

What about refinanced homes?

Debt used to refinance your home qualifies for this exclusion, but only up to the extent that the principal balance of the old mortgage, immediately before the refinancing, would have qualified.

Does this provision apply for the 2007 tax year only?

It applies to qualified debt forgiven in 2007, 2008 or 2009.

If the forgiven debt is excluded from income, do I have to report it on my tax return?

Yes. The amount of debt forgiven must be reported on Form 982 and the Form 982 must be attached to your tax return.

Do I have to complete the entire Form 982?

(http://www.irs.treas.gov/pub/irs-pdf/f982.pdf) Form 982, Reduction of Tax Attributes Due to Discharge of Indebtedness (and Section 1082 Adjustment), is used for other purposes in addition to reporting the exclusion of forgiveness of qualified principal residence indebtedness. If you are using the form only to report the exclusion of forgiveness of qualified principal residence indebtedness as the result of foreclosure on your principal residence, you only need to complete lines 1e and 2. If you kept ownership of your home and modification of the terms of your mortgage resulted in the forgiveness of qualified principal residence indebtedness, complete lines 1e, 2, and 10b. Attach the Form 982 to your tax return.

Where can I get this form?

You can download the form at IRS.gov.

Chapter Seven

So You Want To Do A Short Sale...Top 10 Short Sale Questions Answered:

Number 10

I can't make my house payments but I do have an ability to pay back all or part of the negative equity. Also, I want to preserve my credit score...is a short sale right for me?

Probably not. In cases where the seller can pay back all or part of the negative equity (usually to the 2nd lien holder) it makes sense for them to work out a repayment plan. The lender will then release the lien and allow the home to close.

Number 9

If I pay mortgage insurance but default on my loan, why wouldn't that cover the deficiency amount?

The mortgage insurance is not there for your protection, it only protects your lender.

Number 8

Do I have to have my home 'Approved' by the lender prior to offering it for sale as a short sale?

No. Technically speaking there is no such thing as being 'Short Sale Approved'. The actual approval only happens with an accepted offer.

Number 7

I just missed a payment and I know I will miss more….how long does the foreclosure process take and is there time to do a short sale?

The foreclosure process takes differing times depending on your state. In the Midwest a foreclosure can take over a year. In California it's taking 6+ months. Generally speaking a well-priced short sale being processed by an educated short sale listing agent will sell and close in less than 120 days.

Number 6

Will I still have to pay property taxes if I do a short sale?

Property taxes will always have to be paid as part of any accepted short sale. Whether it's you or the lender depends on their policies and the specific agreement you reach while negotiating the short sale. Your real estate professional will be able to negotiate all or most of your property taxes into the transaction. Many times the lender will cover the entire cost.

Number 5

I owe more than my home is worth and I can't make the payment, do I have to somehow qualify for a short sale?

The simple answer is NO. If someone can't make their payment and they are otherwise insolvent they qualify for a short sale. Note: insolvent simply means their total debts are greater than their assets.

Number 4

Do I have to pay income taxes? I have heard that I will get a 1099. Will the loss the bank takes be treated as a taxable gain to me...the seller? Is this true?

It WAS true, now it's now. Consult your Tax Attorney or Qualified CPA. Very recently the tax law was modified and now most people who do a short sale will have no taxes due.

> The Mortgage Debt Relief Act may make this a non-issue for you! **The Mortgage Debt Relief Act of 2007** generally allows taxpayers to exclude income from the discharge of debt on their principal residence. Debt reduced through mortgage restructuring, as well as mortgage debt forgiven in connection with a foreclosure, qualifies for the relief. This provision applies to debt forgiven in calendar years 2007 through 2012. Up to $2 million of forgiven debt is eligible for this exclusion ($1 million if married filing separately). The exclusion does not apply if the discharge is due to services performed for the lender or any other reason not directly related to a decline in the home's value or the taxpayer's financial condition.
>
> http://www.irs.gov/individuals/article/0,,id=179414,00.html

Number 3

How do you, my listing agent get paid? Who pays you commission? I can't afford to pay that.

The bank will pay the commission along with all the other usual closing costs.

Number 2

Do I have to miss a payment to do a Short Sale?

No. Late last year most major lenders started accepting short sale offers from sellers who have never missed a payment.

Number 1

I want to do a short sale, but I have a 2nd mortgage as well as a first, does this make me ineligible?

No. Both of your lenders will need to be satisfied in some way to complete the short sale. If your first lender will be paid off by the sale, then you just negotiate the terms with the second lender. Most short sales do involve 1st and 2nd lien holder. Real estate professionals who are trained in short sales routinely negotiate transactions involving up to 3 mortgages, as well as delinquent HOA dues and property taxes.

Sample: The following is a sample (from Wells Fargo) of how they handle a potential short sale situation. This is only a sample for your review and understanding. Your own situation may be different and each case is handled individually by each lender.

Contact Letter to Homeowner:

Wells Fargo Financial
4119 121st Street
Urbandale, IA 50323
800-275-9254

Thank you for your interest in our **Home Preservation Program**. By expressing your interest to work with us, you have taken the first step in resolving your current situation. Once we receive the documents requested from you and begin evaluating your financial information worksheet, some of the options that may become available to you include:

- **Repayment Plan** – We can consider a payment plan that will fit your budget and possibly bring your account current by the end of the plan.

- **Loan Modification** –This program may allow the terms of your loan to be adjusted and brought current.

- **Extension** – This payment relief option would bring your account current by putting the past due amount on the end of the loan and allows you to continue making your monthly payment.

- **Home Sales Program** – If your home is currently listed for sale or you are thinking about listing your home with a realtor, Wells Fargo Financial has a team of sales specialists that will work with you and your agent. This team will make the sale process flow as smoothly as possible. If the home's market value is less than the total amount owed, the sales specialist will work closely with you and the realtor to help you resolve this issue in the best way possible.

In order for us to get started right away, we need a few documents from you. It is extremely important that the financial information you provide is complete and as accurate as possible to avoid delays in evaluation. You will need to print out, complete and return the enclosed documents. If you are in a position to bring your account current without our assistance, please call us at (800) 275-9254, Monday through Friday, 8 AM to 9 PM, Central Time and Saturday 8AM to 7PM, Central Time.

Please fax* or mail your completed package to:

Wells Fargo Financial Real Estate
Attention: Home Preservation Department
MAC F4012-011
4143 121st Street
Urbandale, IA 50323
Fax: (877) 455-9956

*Your faxed information is secure and will be kept strictly confidential.

The laws of some states require us to inform you that this communication is an attempt to collect a debt and any information obtained will be used for that purpose.

Wells Fargo Financial
4119 121st Street
Urbandale, IA 50323
800-275-9254

Sample Items In A Typical (In This Case Wells Fargo) Short Sale Package:

1: Detailed Hardship Letter

Account Number:
Name:
Best Number to Contact you:
Best Time of the Day to Call You:
Cell Phone #
Check here □ For Consent to Call

Please explain to us in writing your reason for delinquency. Please be very specific in the events that have happened as this will be included in the decision of the hardship program.

1. What caused you to get behind on your mortgage payments?

2. Approximately, when did this hardship occur?

3. Is this an ongoing hardship, and if so, are there any additional monthly expenses associated with the problem?

4. In regards to your monthly mortgage payment(s), how much extra can you pay to bring your account up to date?

5. Is the home up for sale? If yes what is your realtor name and number?

6. Homeowner's insurance current or expired? Agent name and contact number?

7. Property taxes are they current or past due? If past due, what is the amount and are you on a workout plan with the county to resolve them?

_____

Customer Signature

_____

Date

_____

Co-Borrower Signature Date

2. Financial Information Sheet

Borrower's Name(s) Account Number:

Name: Social Security Number:

Name: Social Security Number:

Home Phone Number: Work Phone Numbers:

Other numbers (cell phone, etc):

Property Address: circle one: primary residence or rental property

Mailing Address (if different than property address) **Own** How Long:

Street Address, City, State, Zip Code

Present Employer

(borrower) Date of Employment:

Present Employer (co-borrower)

Date of Employment:

Status: full time or part time:

Monthly Income Information: (Note: please provide two most recent pay stubs.)

Description Income (borrower) Income (Co-borrower) Total

Net Salary/Wages

Commission/Bonuses

Other Income (explain)

Total Net Income

Assets

Estimated Value Comments

Automobile (Make and Model)

Wells Fargo Financial Secured Property:

Checking Accounts

Other Real Estate (explain)

Savings/Money Market Accounts

IRA/Keogh Accounts

401K/ESOP Accounts

Stocks/Bonds, CD's

Life Insurance (Cash Value)

Other

Property Taxes

Homeowner's Insurance

Automobile Payment

Automobile Payment

Liabilities

Monthly Payment Balance Due

Company

Name

First Mortgage Payment

Second Mortgage Payment

Other Mortgage or Rent

Payment

Monthly Payment Balance Due

Child Care Expenses

Alimony/Child Support

Student Loan Payment

Assets	Liabilities
Credit Card Payment	Medical Expenses
Personal Loan Payment	Transportation Expense
Utilities (explain)	Miscellaneous Expense
Health Insurance	(explain)

The laws of some states require us to inform you that this communication is an attempt to collect a debt and any information obtained will be used for that purpose.

3. Other Required Documents

Current income documents are needed to accurately assess your financial situation to determine the best solution to fit your unique needs. Please immediately return all documents that would correspond to your current sources of income.

Wage Earner:

☐ Previous 2 years W-2's

☐ Completed Information Disclosure (form enclosed)

☐ Two most recent pay stubs

Business for Self:

☐ Previous 2 years signed tax returns

☐ Year to date profit and loss statement

☐ IRS Forms 1099/W-2

Fixed Income:

☐ Current SSI/Disability award letters

☐ Pension annuity statement

☐ Recent bank statements showing deposits

If you have other sources of income that you wish to be included please provide documentation. Additional items may be requested upon further review of your documents.

4. Information Disclosure Authorization

To Whom It May Concern:

I/We Hereby Authorize you to Release for Verification Purposes, Information Requested on the Attached Forms Concerning:

___X___ Employment history, dates, title, income, hours worked, etc.

___X___ Banking, checking, and savings accounts records

___X___ Mortgage loan rating and information (opening date, high credit, payment

amount, loan balance, payment record, payoff, etc.)

___X___ Any information deemed necessary in connection with a consumer credit
report for a real estate transaction

THIS INFORMATION IS FOR CONFIDENTIAL USE IN COMPILING A MORTGAGE LOAN CREDIT REPORT. A PHOTOGRAPHIC, CARBON, OR FAXED COPY OF THIS AUTHORIZATION (BEING A COPY OF THE SIGNATURE(S) OF THE UNDERSIGNED) MAY BE DEEMED TO BE THE EQUIVALENT OF THE ORIGINAL AND MAY BE USED AS A DUPLICATE ORIGINAL. YOUR PROMPT REPLY WILL BE GREATLY APPRECIATED.

THANK YOU FOR YOUR COOPERATION,

_____

Signature   Date   Social Security Number

_____

Signature   Date   Social Security Number

Chapter Eight

But, I Thought Rates Were Falling…Won't That Help Me?

T he Federal Reserve has been lowering rates to bail out the economy. Does this mean that mortgage rates will fall?

In some cases yes in most cases no…read on.

Let's start with the 30-year fixed rate mortgage. The 30-year fixed rate mortgage is not tied to short-term treasuries. Fixed mortgage rates are tied to long-term bond yields that move based on the outlook for the economy and inflation. True, even as the Fed has lowered rates, the 30-year fixed has come down, but that's because of the outlook for slower economic growth in the months ahead. While the decline in treasury yields has helped push mortgage rates lower, the decline in long term rates hasn't been in lockstep thanks to the fact that these mortgages are securitized and sold on the global market. Investors now demand a higher risk premium on these mortgages due to higher delinquencies and foreclosures.

Next let's take a look at 7 and 5-1 Adjustable Rate Mortgages (ARMs) Yes, this is good news if your 5-year (or 7 year) ARM is pegged to a treasury index. So if you're facing a reset on, say, a $200,000 loan, you're now getting a payment increase of about $150 a month, as opposed to $370 a month, which you would have had before the Fed started cutting rates.

Do the Fed Rate Drops Help Sub-Prime mortgage Holders?

Nope. Unfortunately if you have a sub-prime ARM it is more than likely pegged to LIBOR, which has moved in the opposite direction. Because of the liquidity issues in global financial markets, LIBOR rates have actually increased at the same time that treasury and other benchmark yields have been declining, so the Fed lowering rates today would not help too many sub-prime mortgage holders.

How are Home Equity Lines of Credit Affected?

How about my Home Equity Line of Credit (HELOC): Yes, if you have that home equity line of credit that you used to renovate your bathroom/kitchen recently, then when the Fed lowers rates, your rate comes down as well. That's because HELOCs are predominantly pegged to the prime rate, which moves in step with the Federal Reserve.

Chapter Nine

Life After Short Sale…When You Want To Buy A Home Again…It's FHA To The Rescue!

What is an FHA Loan?

Get ready for FHA loans to become the best choice for EVEN in the high priced areas like California!

It's now possible to get a FHA Mortgage in certain parts of the country for over $700,000!

You Must Know How FHA Loans Work:

First, it's important to understand that FHA is not only for first time home buyers, anyone can sign up for an FHA loan, as long as you don't have more than one FHA Loan at a time.

Your job is to establish a relationship with an FHA approved lender. Not all lenders hold this qualification.

Little Known SECRETS of FHA Loans:

FHA can help clients with blemished credit history. New programs are coming out that will allow borrowers with credit score in the high 500s buy a home…and….

- **Bankruptcy**. You can obtain an FHA loan two years from the date of your bankruptcy discharge, as long as you've maintained good credit since your debts were discharged.

- **Foreclosure**. If you keep your credit in excellent shape since a foreclosure, an FHA loan will be available to you two years from the final date of your foreclosure.

Ultra Competitive Rates & Terms

- There is little or no adjustment to the interest rate for an FHA loan, as the rates vary within .125 percent of a conventional loan.

- Mortgage insurance is funded into the loan, meaning a premium of 1.5% is added to the loan balance instead of being paid out-of-pocket. In addition, a small portion for the mortgage insurance premium is added to the monthly payment, but it is far less than private mortgage insurance premiums.

- Borrowers can finance 97% of the purchase price and put down 3 percent. In some instances, when combined with other types of loans, the down payment can be zero.

- Allowable debt ratios are higher than the debt-ratio limits imposed for conventional loans.

- Borrowers can get up to 6% back from the seller to help with all of their closing costs.

Forget what you thought you knew about FHA...

At one point, FHA repair demands were so excessive that sellers would discount the list price to buyers who would agree to obtain conventional loans over FHA loans. Today the requirements appear more reasonable.

- You can purchase a home in need of repairs and finance the repair costs with the mortgage. This way you can make the necessary repairs immediately without having to come up with the money yourself.

- You can purchase manufactured homes and condominiums with a FHA loan.

- You can finance the cost of energy-efficient repairs with the mortgage.

- Defective roofs that leak still need to be replaced but an older roof does not necessitate replacement if it doesn't leak. A roofing certification is acceptable in most cases.

- Windows that stick upon opening or have cracked panes do not require replacement.

- FHA appraisals do not take the place of a home inspection, and never have. Buyers should still obtain a professional home inspection.

It's time to take advantage of the return of the FHA loan! It's about to become significantly better than before, with higher limits and an easier appraisal process.

For more information on various types of FHA loans, check here or call your trusted real estate advisor: www.fha.com.

Chapter Ten

Something You Should Know. The Death Of The Heloc…. Millions Of Homeowners Shut Out

Most major lenders are freezing withdrawals from Home Equity Lines of Credit (HELOCs) – and I don't want you to be caught off guard by this development. If you were planning on using your HELOC for spring home improvements or college tuition chances are the money has been shut off.

You should be aware that the lender retains the right to suspend or reduce the line of credit available if your property value falls below the appraised value used to originate the loan. Lenders are actively assessing properties and then suspending access for account holders who have seen a downward slide in their home value. Many of our students who do BPOs are reporting to us a dramatic increase in BPO requests from lenders for this reason.

From Countrywide… sent to borrowers:

'Important message about your loan: At Countrywide Home Loans we are committed to helping customers sustain homeownership. As part of the commitment, and in keeping with its sound risk-management and responsible lending practices, Countrywide Home Loan is reviewing and analyzing home equity lines of credit in its servicing portfolio.

We believe that the decline in the value of your property, from its original appraised value at the time your loan was made is significant. In accordance with the terms of your Home Equity Credit Line Agreement and Disclosure Statement (Agreement), we have elected to suspend further draws against your account as of the Effective Date above.'

On Friday, the Los Angeles Times reported that Countrywide notified many homeowners they've lost their right to borrow against their credit lines:

'Tens of thousands of homeowners with home equity lines of credit are getting a rude surprise: They've been told by their lender that they can no longer take money out on their credit lines because sinking home prices have left them with little or no equity.

Among the lenders taking such action is Countrywide Financial Corp., which sent 122,000 letters to customers last week telling them they could no longer borrow against their credit lines. In some cases, according to the company, the borrowers are now "upside down" — the total debt on the home exceeds the market value of the property.

Calabasas-based Countrywide, the nation's largest mortgage lender, says it uses computer modeling that factors in changes in home prices to determine which customers will have their money tap shut off.'

If there was any question that consumers were feeling the pinch before…just wait until they are told that their homes are worth LESS than what they owe. Or in the words of Countrywide…"Significantly Less". Think that will have an effect on the economy. Think this will make consumers feel more confident about housing?

[Intentionally Blank]

Appendices

Appendix A:

HAFA (Home Affordable Foreclosure Alternatives)

Information and Forms:

http://timandjulieharris.com/hafaforms/

http://timandjulieharris.com/wp-content/uploads/2010/10/HAFA-Definition-Spreadsheet.pdf

Lenders who are participating in HAFA:

Allstate Mortgage Loans & Investments, Inc.

American Home Mortgage Servicing, Inc.

AMS Servicing, LLC

Aurora Loan Services LLC

Bank of America, N.A.

Bank United

Bay Federal Credit Union

Bayview Loan Servicing, LLC

CCO Mortgage

Carrington Mortgage Services, LLC

Central Florida Educators Federal Credit Union

Central Jersey Federal Credit Union

CitiMortgage, Inc.

Citizens First Wholesale Mortgage Co.

Countrywide Home Loans Servicing LP

CUC Mortgage Corporation

DuPage Credit Union

EMC Mortgage Corporation

Farmers State Bank

First Bank

First Federal Savings and Loan Association of Port Angeles

First Keystone Bank

Franklin Credit Management Corporation

Glass City Federal Credit Union

GMAC Mortgage LLC

Great Lakes Credit Union

Green Tree Servicing LLC

Harleysville National Bank & Trust Company

Hillsdale County National Bank

HomEq Servicing

Home Financing Center Inc.

Home Loan Services, Inc.

Horicon Bank

IBM Southeast Employees Federal Credit Union

IC Federal Credit Union

J.P. Morgan Chase Bank, NA

Lake City Bank

Lake National Bank

Litton Loan Servicing

Los Alamos National Bank

Marix Servicing, LLC

Members Mortgage Company, Inc

Mission Federal Credit Union

Members Mortgage Company, Inc.

Metropolitan National Bank

MorEquity, Inc.

Mortgage Center, LLC

Mortgage Clearing Corporation

National City Bank

Nationstar Mortgage LLC

Oakland Municipal Credit Union

Ocwen Financial Corporation, Inc.

OneWest Bank

ORNL Federal Credit Union

PennyMac Loan Services, LLC

PNC Bank, National Association

Purdue Employees Federal Credit Union

Qlending, Inc.

Quantum Servicing Corporation

RG Mortgage Corporation

Residential Credit Solutions

RoundPoint Mortgage Servicing Corporation

Saxon Mortgage Services

Schools Financial Credit Union

SEFCU

Select Portfolio Servicing

Servis One Inc., dba BSI Financial Services, Inc

ShoreBank

Stanford Federal Credit Union

Technology Credit Union

United Bank Mortgage Corporation

U.S. Bank National Association

Vantium Capital, Inc.

Wachovia Mortgage, FSB

Wachovia Bank, NA

Wells Fargo Bank, NA

Wescom Central Credit Union

Wilshire Credit Corporation

Yadkin Valley Bank

Appendix B:

Lender/Servicer Loss Mitigation Phone Numbers & Contact Information:

Your lender may be on this list. If they are NOT, call your trusted real estate professional, or ask us for a referral: 866 422 9497. Your agent can get the ball rolling, even if you're just looking for answers from your lender about your mortgage.

ABM AMRO Mortgage (800) 783-8900
Web: https://www.mortgage.com/C3/application.bus

Accredited Home Lenders (877) 683-4466

AMC Mortgage Services (Also handles loans originated by Ameriquest and Argent) (800) 211-6926 https://www.myamcloan.com/malwebapp/begin.do

American Home Mortgage Corp. (877) 304-3100

Ameriquest Mortgage (Debt collection — see AMC Mortgage Services) (800) 211-6926

Aurora Loan Services (Debt collection) (800) 550-0508

Beneficial (800) 333-5848

Central Pacific Bank (800) 342-8422

Charter One (800) 234-6002

Chase (800) 548-7912

Loss Mitigation (877) 838-1882 ext 52195. The Number you will be directed to after you give your loan number: (866) 665-

Chase Home Finance (800) 848-9136 (customer service) (858) 605-2181 (delinquency customer service)

Chevy Chase Bank (800) 933-9100 https://chaseonline.chase.com/chaseonline/logon/sso_logon.jsp?fromLoc=ALL&LOB=COLLogon

Chase Manhattan Mortgage
(800) 446-8939 (Ohio Servicing Center)
(800) 526-0072 (Florida Servicing Center)
(800) 527-3040 x533 (Florida Servicing Center)

Chevy Chase Bank (800) 933-9100 https://www.chevychasebank.com/htm/payment.html (Payment Addresses)

Citi Ficial

Citimortgage (800) 283-7918

Ditech (800) 852-0656 (800) 449-8582

Downey Financial Corp. (800) 824-6902, ext. 6696

Deutsche Bank National Call Number on Mortgage Statement

EMC (800) 723-3004

EverBank (800) 669-7724 ext. 4730

Equity One (Debt collection) (866) 361-3460

First Horizon Home Loans (800) 489-2966

Fifth Third Bank (800) 375-1745 Option 3

First Merit Bank (888) 728-9931

Flagstar Bank (800) 968-7700, ext. 9780

Fremont Investment & Loan (866) 484-0291

GMAC Mortgage (800) 850-4622

GreenPoint Mortgage Funding (800) 784-5566, ext. 5383*

Green Tree (877) 816-9125

Homecomings Financial (800) 799-9250

HomeEq Mortgage Servicing (Debt collection) (866) 822-1471

Household Finance (A HSBC Co.) (800) 333-5848

Household Mortgage (800) 333-4489

HSBC Mortgage (800) 338-6441
Default Resolution Team (if long term problem)
2929 Walden Avenue
Depew, NY 14043
(888) 648-3124 Loss Mit
(732) 352-7519 Fax
Web: http://us.hsbc.com/personal/mortgage/existing/difficulties.asp

Huntington National Bank (800) 323-4695

Indymac Bank (877) 736-5556
C/O Loan Resolution Department
P.O Box 7014
Pasadena, CA 91107
(Monday – Friday 6:15am-7:15pm. (Pacific Time)
Web: https://www.indymacbank.com/contactus/loanResolution.asp

Irwin Mortgage (888) 218-1988

Litton Loan Servicing (800) 999-8501 or (800) 548-8665
https://www.littonloan.com/index.asp

NationStar Mortgage (888) 850-9398* Press 0 for operator

New Century Financial Now Carrington Mortgage Services (800) 790-9502
or (877) 206-9904

Ocwen Federal Bank (800) 746-2936 or (877) 596-8560
http://www.ocwencustomers.com/csc_fa.cfm

PHH Mortgage (Formerly Cendant) (800) 257-0460
For borrowers facing possible delinquency: (800) 330-0423*
For borrowers in the foreclosure process: (800) 750-2518

Saxon (800) 665-7367

Select Portfolio Servicing (888) 818-6032

SkyBank (800) 290-3359

Sun Trust Mortgage (800) 634-7928
https://www.suntrustmortgage.com/generalquestions.asp#

Third Federal Savings (888) 844-7333

US Bank (800) 365-7900

Wachovia Bank of Delaware (866) 642-8608

Washington Mutual (866) 926-8937 or (888) 453-3102 or (800) 478-0036 or
(800) 254-3677

Waterfirld Mortgage (800) 957-7245
Fax: (260) 459-5390 saveyourhome@waterfield.com

Wells Fargo (877) 216-8448 or (866) 261-5642 or (800)766-0987 or (800) 678-7986 for payment https://www.wellsfargo.com/mortgage/account/

Wendover Financial Services Corporation (800) 934-1081 or (800) 436-1022
http://www.wendover.com/borrowers.html

Wilshire Credit Corporation (888) 502-0100
http://www.wfsg.com/borrower/borrower.aspx

Appendix C:

What's the difference between Short Sale vs Short Payoff?

In our current real estate environment it is crucial that to fully understand the difference between a "**Short Sale**" and a "**Short Payoff**".

A **Short Sale** is where the lender or investor agrees to accept an amount less than actual owed on the property.

The **Criteria for a Short Sale** are that the borrower demonstrates a verifiable long term hardship.

A **Short Payoff** is when the lender agrees to release the lien (their interest) on the property and allow the property to be "conveyed" to a new owner. The lender agrees to accept less than the amount owed on the property to release the lien however they extend a certain amount of "credit" to the borrower in the form of an unsecured line of credit or promissory note.

The Criteria for a Short Payoff – The mortgage is current, the borrower has great credit, the borrower had and can demonstrate the ability to pay off the debt.

When would you request a Short Payoff? – You would request a short payoff when the home has lost value dramatically and you do not have the ability to pay the large amount to get completely out of the property.

Note – Not all lenders will allow for a Short Payoff, however you will never know if you never ask.

Advantages of a Short Pay-Off:

- You are able to move out of the property and get on with your life.

- You SHOULD receive no negative feedback on your credit.

- You may obtain a lower interest rate on the loan. Sometimes 1-2%.

If for some crazy reason your ability to pay changes and your client are not able to pay on the note, the credit ramifications are significantly smaller.

How to apply for a short payoff:

1. If possible call the lender and ask them if they will accept a short payoff. Remember you may need to talk to a supervisor or to loss mitigation directly.

2. Put together your package, this is the same information as your short sale package, however the goal is to show the lender the ability to pay not the inability to pay.

3. Do not accept the first no as the answer, and never paint a lender or servicer with a broad brush. Remember most lenders do not work with just one investor, lenders sell their loans to different investors so if Bank of America says no today that does not mean no tomorrow.

Man in the Arena

*"It is not the critic who counts: not the man who points out how the strong man stumbles or where the doer of deeds could have done better. The credit belongs to the man who is actually in the arena, whose face is marred by dust and sweat and blood, who strives valiantly, who errs and comes up short again and again, because there is no effort without error or shortcoming, but who knows the great enthusiasms, the great devotions, who spends himself for a worthy cause; who, at the best, knows, in the end, the triumph of high achievement, and who, at the worst, if he fails, at least he fails while daring greatly, so that his place shall never be with those cold and timid souls who knew neither victory nor **defeat.** "*

Theodore Roosevelt

Appendix D:

The Complete State-by-State Guidebook on the most Common Foreclosure Procedures

This section is written for the purpose of providing current information in regard to the topics as set forth in the text. It is not the intention of any author or publisher herein, to provide the reader with specific legal, financial, tax, accounting or professional advice. Each state is different and applicable laws, regulations and terminology for related subjects may vary in different jurisdictions. Considerable efforts are made to provide the reader with timely and accurate information; however there are no guarantees. Therefore, if expert assistance and advice is required, the reader should always seek the services of a competent professional. The authors are not attorneys or accountants.

The following information was compiled by:

www.HarrisRealEstateUniversity.com

If you have any questions please visit our site. The chart below is courtesy of RealtyTrac.

State	Judicial	Non-Judicial	Comments	Process Period (Days)	Sale Publication (Days)	Redemption Period (Days)	Sale/NTS
Alabama	•	•		49-74	21	365	Trustee
Alaska	•	•		105	65	365*	Trustee
Arizona	•	•		90+	41	30-180*	Trustee
Arkansas	•	•		70	30	365*	Trustee
California	•	•		117	21	365*	Trustee
Colorado	•	•		145	60	None	Trustee
Connecticut	•	•		62	NA	Court Decides	Court
Delaware	•	•		170-210	60-90	None	Sheriff
District of Columbia	•	•		47	18	None	Trustee
Florida	•	•		135	NA	None	Court
Georgia	•	•		37	32	None	Trustee
Hawaii	•	•		220	60	None	Trustee
Idaho	•	•		150	45	365	Trustee
Illinois	•	•		300	NA	90	Court
Iowa	•	•		160	30	20	Sheriff
Kansas	•	•		130	21	365	Sheriff
Kentucky	•	•		147	NA	365	Court
Louisiana	•	•		180	NA	None	Sheriff
Maine	•	•		240	30	90	Court
Maryland	•	•		46	30	Court Decides	Court
Massachusetts	•	•		75	41	None	Court
Michigan	•	•		60	30	30-365	Sheriff
Minnesota	•	•		90-100	7	1825	Sheriff
Mississippi	•	•		90	30	None	Trustee
Missouri	•	•		60	10	365	Trustee
Montana	•	•		150	50	None	Trustee
Nebraska	•	•		142	NA	None	Sheriff
Nevada	•	•		116	80	None	Trustee
New Hampshire	•	•		59	24	None	Trustee
New Jersey	•	•		270	NA	10	Sheriff
New Mexico	•	•		180	NA	30-270	Court
New York	•	•		445	NA	None	Court
North Carolina	•	•		110	25	None	Sheriff

State	Judicial	Non-Judicial	Comments	Process Period (Days)	Sale Publication (Days)	Redemption Period (Days)	Sale/NTS
North Dakota	•	•		150	NA	180-365	Sheriff
Ohio	•	•		217	NA	None	Sheriff
Oklahoma	•	•		186	NA	None	Sheriff
Oregon	•	•		150	30	180	Trustee
Pennsylvania	•	•		270	NA	None	Sheriff
Rhode Island	•	•		62	21	None	Trustee
South Carolina	•	•		150	NA	None	Court
South Dakota	•	•		150	23	30-365	Sheriff
Tennessee	•	•		40-45	20-25	730	Trustee
Texas	•	•		27	NA	None	Trustee
Utah	•	•		142	NA	Court Decides	Trustee
Vermont	•	•		95	NA	180-365	Court
Virginia	•	•		45	14-28	None	Trustee
Washington	•	•		135	90	None	Trustee
West Virginia	•	•		60-90	30-60	None	Trustee
Wisconsin	•	•		290	NA	365	Sheriff
Wyoming	•	•		60	25	90-365	Sheriff

Judicial Only Mouseover the symbol to view state-specific comments

Alabama Foreclosure Laws

The foreclosure process varies somewhat from state to state, and depends primarily on whether the state uses mortgages or deeds of trust for the purchase of real property. Generally, states that use mortgages conduct judicial foreclosures; states that use deeds of trust conduct non-judicial foreclosures. The principal difference between the two is that the judicial procedure requires court action on a foreclosed home.

To foreclose in accordance with the judicial procedure, a lender must prove that the mortgagor (borrower/homeowner) is in default. Once the lender has exhausted its attempts to resolve the default with the homeowner, the next step is to contact an attorney to pursue court action. The attorney contacts the mortgagor to try to resolve the default. If the mortgagor is unable to pay off the default, the attorney files a lis pendens (lawsuit pending) with the court. The lis pendens gives notice to the public that a pending action has been filed against the mortgagor. The purpose of the action is to provide evidence of a default and get the court's approval to initiate foreclosure.

Non-judicial foreclosures are based on deeds of trust that contain the power of sale clause. The clause enables the trustee to initiate a mortgage foreclosure sale without having to go to court. The trustee is typically required to issue a notice of default and notify the trustor (borrower/homeowner) accordingly about the default status. If the trustor does not respond, the trustee then initiates the steps for conducting the mortgage foreclosure sale of the home.

Expected Timeline: One to three months **Security Instrument:** Mortgage or Deed of Trust **Type of Process:** Judicial or Nonjudicial **Protections for Service members:** Ala. Code § 31-12-1 to 31-12-10 **Time to Respond:** Foreclosing party required to publish notice in newspaper of general circulation for four weeks. There is no requirement that the homeowner be served a copy by mail. **Reinstatement Period:** None. **Protections for High-Cost Mortgages:** None. **Redemption Period:** Twelve months after sale in judicial foreclosure. **Eviction Process:** No specific notification process. **Deficiency Judgments:** Allowed in judicial foreclosure. Not allowed in no judicial foreclosure. **Limits on Deficiency Judgments:** Deficiency judgments are possible. No limits. **Cash Exempted in Bankruptcy:** None. **State Statutes:** Ala. Code § 35-10-1 to 35-10-30, 6-5-247 to 6-5-256.

Alaska Foreclosure Laws

Expected Timeline: Three to four months **Security Instrument:** Mortgage or Deed of Trust **Type of Process:** Judicial or Non judicial. Non judicial foreclosure are most common. **Protections for Service members:** Alaska Stat. § 26.05.135 **Time to Respond:** Notice must be sent not less than thirty days after default and more less than three months before sheriff sale of the property. **Reinstatement Period:** Anytime before foreclosure auction. Lender may refuse to allow reinstatement if this is the third notice of default and notice of sale. **Protections for High-Cost Mortgages:** None. **Redemption Period:** None. **Eviction Process:** New owner must serve notice to quit on former owners and may bring civil lawsuit to gain possession. **Deficiency Judgments:** Not allowed in Non judicial foreclosure. **Limits on Deficiency Judgments:**

Deficiency judgments are not allowed if the foreclosure is by power of sale (Non judicial foreclosure). **Cash Exempted in Bankruptcy:** $1,750 for single person; $3,500 for married couples. **State Statutes:** Alaska Stat. § 34.20.070.

Arizona Foreclosure Laws

Expected Timeline: Three to four months **Security Instrument:** Deed of Trust most common in Arizona **Type of Process:** Non judicial foreclosure most common. Judicial foreclosure used under a mortgage or if trustee chooses it under a deed of trust. **Protections for Service members:** Ariz. Rev. Stat. Ann. § 6-1260(L) **Time to Respond:** Notice of sale must be recorded at least ninety days before sheriff sale. Homeowners must be notified via certified mail within five days of recording of notice of sale. **Reinstatement Period:** Allowed until day before auction date in Non judicial foreclosure. Reinstatement allowed anytime before complaint is filed in judicial foreclosure. **Protections for High-Cost Mortgages:** None. **Redemption Period:** None under Non judicial foreclosure. Six months after auction date under judicial foreclosure, but only for properties not abandoned and not agricultural land. **Eviction Process:** New owner demands that previous owners leave. No specific time line. New owner may go to court to sue for a writ of possession. **Deficiency Judgments:** Not allowed in Non judicial foreclosures. Allowed in judicial if deficiency judgment lawsuit is filed within ninety days of foreclosure auction. **Limits on Deficiency Judgments:** No deficiency judgment on a purchase money mortgage for one- or two-family properties on less than two and a half acres. A deficiency may be allowed if a court decides the owners committed waste. **Cash Exempted in Bankruptcy:** $150 **State Statutes:** Ariz. Rev. Stat. § 33-741 to 33-749, 33-801 to 33-821, 12-1281 to 12-1283, 12-1566.

Arkansas Foreclosure Laws

Expected Timeline: Four to five months **Security Instrument:** Mortgage or Deed of Trust **Type of Process:** Judicial or Non judicial **Protections for Service members:** Ark. Code Ann. § 12-62-718 **Time to Respond:** Foreclosing party must provide thirty days notice of default and intent to sell. Notice of sale must also be published for four weeks before sale date. Notice must be posted at the courthouse and any website where local legal notices are routinely posted. **Reinstatement Period:** Allowed up to date of foreclosure auction. **Protections for High-Cost Mortgages:** Ark. Code Ann. § 23-53-01 to 106 **Redemption Period:** None allowed in Non judicial foreclosure. One year from date of sale in judicial foreclosure. **Eviction Process:** No specific timeline for eviction. **Deficiency Judgments:** Allowed for up to the market value of the property less the foreclosure auction proceeds. Lawsuit must be filed within one year of auction date. **Limits on Deficiency Judgments:** Lawsuit for deficiency must be brought within one year from the date of the public sale. Deficiency limited to amount of indebtedness less fair market value; or deficiency limited to amount of indebtedness less sales price of home. **Cash Exempted in Bankruptcy:** $11,000 for single person; $22,000 for married couple. **State Statutes:** Ark. Code Ann. § 18-49-101 to 18-49-106, 18-50-101 to 18-50-116.

California Foreclosure Laws

Expected Timeline: Around four months **Security Instrument:** Deed of Trust **Type of Process:** Judicial or Non judicial. The vast majority of foreclosures are Non judicial. **Protections for Service members:** Cal. Mil. & Vet. Code § 400 to 409.13 **Time to Respond:** Homeowners must be contact by bank at least thirty days before notice of default is sent. Notice of default is ninety days; notice of sale twenty-one days. **Reinstatement Period:** Allowed any time up to five days before sheriff sale. **Protections for High-Cost Mortgages:** Cal. Fin. Code § 4973 and 4978 **Redemption Period:** There is no redemption if the deficiency judgment is waived or prohibited in the case. **Eviction Process:** There is no redemption if the deficiency judgment is waived or prohibited in the case. **Deficiency Judgments:** Not allowed in Non judicial foreclosures. **Limits on Deficiency Judgments:** No deficiency allowed under judicial foreclosure unless there is no redemption period, and no deficiencies are allowed under Non judicial foreclosure. Deficiencies that are allowed are limited by fair market value of property. **Cash Exempted in Bankruptcy:** Up to $22,000 **State Statutes:** Cal. Civ. Code § 2924 to 2924l.

Colorado Foreclosure Laws

Expected Timeline: Two to five months **Security Instrument:** Mortgage or Deed of Trust. Deeds of trust are much more common. **Type of Process:** Non judicial most common in Colorado. Judicial will be used if a mortgage is used instead of a deed of trust. **Protections for Service members:** None. **Time to**

Respond: Public trustee will mail notice within twenty days of recording notice of sale and 45-60 days before scheduled sale date. Notice of sale must be published for four weeks before sale. Notices mailed to homeowners must include information on reinstatement rights. **Reinstatement Period:** Allowed until noon on date of sheriff sale. Notice must be given to lender of intent to reinstate no later than fifteen days before sale. **Protections for High-Cost Mortgages:** None. **Redemption Period:** None. **Eviction Process:** Former owner served with court proceeding and has 3-5 days to respond. After response is filed, a hearing will be held before the court within two weeks. If former owners lose, eviction can be scheduled within days. **Deficiency Judgments:** Allowed if suit is filed within 75 days of sheriff sale. If house was sold for less than market value, deficiency suit may be defeated. **Limits on Deficiency Judgments:** Deficiency is allowed, but homeowners may claim the house sold for less than the fair market value as a defense against this. **Cash Exempted in Bankruptcy:** None. **State Statutes:** Colo Rev. Stat. § 38-38-100.3 to 38-38-114.

Connecticut Foreclosure Laws

Expected Timeline: Five to six months **Security Instrument:** Mortgage **Type of Process:** Judicial mostly. Lenders can request strict foreclosure, where court transfers title directly without sheriff sale. **Protections for Service members:** Conn. Gen. Stat. § 36a-737 **Time to Respond:** Homeowners have 20-30 days to respond after the foreclosure lawsuit is filed. **Reinstatement Period:** None. **Protections for High-Cost Mortgages:** None. **Redemption Period:** Court may set redemption period in addition to setting sale date. **Eviction Process:** Judge can order immediate eviction of former owners after title is transferred. **Deficiency Judgments:** May be obtained within thirty days of redemption period expiring. **Limits on Deficiency Judgments:** Deficiencies are allowed if they are pursued within thirty days of the end of the redemption period. **Cash Exempted in Bankruptcy:** $11,000 for single person, $22,000 for married couples. **State Statutes:** Conn. Gen. Stat. § 49-1 to 49-31.

Delaware Foreclosure Laws

Expected Timeline: Three to seven months **Security Instrument:** Mortgage **Type of Process:** Judicial foreclosure **Protections for Service**

members: None. **Time to Respond:** Twenty days to respond with why a foreclosure should not proceed to an Order to Show Cause. Homeowners receive a ten day notice of sale after judgment in the lawsuit. **Reinstatement Period:** None. **Protections for High-Cost Mortgages:** None. **Redemption Period:** Able to redeem until court confirms sheriff sale. **Eviction Process:** New owner can file summar eviction lawsuit five days after the auction. Eviction hearing will be held within 5-30 days. Eviction will be ordered after hearing if former owners do not show up or lose. See Del. Code Ann. tit. 10, § 5703-5708. **Deficiency Judgments:** May be obtained if bank files separate lawsuit after foreclosure judgment. **Limits on Deficiency Judgments:** Deficiency judgment allowed if lawsuit filed on note. Not allowed in judicial foreclosure proceedings. **Cash Exempted in Bankruptcy:** $500 for single person, $1,000 for married couple. **State Statutes:** Del. Code Ann. tit. 10, § 5061.

Washington, D.C. Foreclosure Laws

Expected Timeline: Two to four months **Security Instrument:** Deed of trust **Type of Process:** Non judicial **Protections for Service members:** None. **Time to Respond:** Lender must send thirty day notice of sale to homeowner via registered or certified mail. Thirty day notice begins when homeowners receive notice. A copy of the notice must also be mailed to the Washington, DC mayor. **Reinstatement Period:** Allowed up to five days before the foreclosure auction. **Protections for High-Cost Mortgages:** None. **Redemption Period:** None. **Eviction Process:** No specific timeline for eviction. **Deficiency Judgments:** May be obtained by filing a lawsuit after the sheriff sale. **Limits on Deficiency Judgments:** Deficiency judgments are allowed. If one is sought under judicial foreclosure proceedings, it may be entered in the foreclosure lawsuit. **Cash Exempted in Bankruptcy:** $11,000 for single person, $22,000 for married couple. **State Statutes:** D.C. Code Ann. § 42-815.

Florida Foreclosure Laws

Expected Timeline: About five months **Security Instrument:** Mortgage **Type of Process:** Judicial **Protections for Service members:** Fla. Stat. Ann. § 250.5201 to 250.5205 **Time to Respond:** Notice of lawsuit not required under Florida law, but most mortgages provide for notice. If lender asks for Order to Show Cause, homeowners have 21 days to respond after personal service or 31 days after notice by publication. Notice of sale must be published for two consecutive weeks at least five days before auction date. **Reinstatement Period:** Allowed for high cost loans. **Protections for High-Cost Mortgages:** Florida Fiair Lending Act, Fla. Stat. Ann. § 494.0078, 494.00794 **Redemption Period:** Available under certificate of sale is filed by clerk of court. **Eviction Process:** New owner files civil complaint to gain possession of property. Former owners have five days to respond. **Deficiency Judgments:** Allowed if owners are personally served with lawsuit. Lenders who made loan to homeowners for the purchase of the property and buy the property back at the sheriff sale cannot sue for a deficiency. Courts have great flexibility in amount of deficiency to award. **Limits on Deficiency Judgments:** Homeowners entitled to jury trial in deficiency case. Bank must have in-hand service on borrowers to include deficiency action in the foreclosure lawsuit. **Cash Exempted in Bankruptcy:** $1,000 for single person, $2,000 for married couples. **State Statutes:** Fla. Stat. Ann. § 702.01, 45.031.

Georgia Foreclosure Laws

Expected Timeline: About two months **Security Instrument:** Mortgage or Deed of Trust. Deed of trust is more common. **Type of Process:** Judicial or non judicial. Non judicial is more common in Georgia foreclosures. **Protections for Service members:** Ga. Code Ann. § 46-5-8 **Time to Respond:** Notice of sale must be mailed to homeowners within 15 days of auction. Additional notices in local newspaper publications may be required. **Reinstatement Period:** High cost loans may be reinstated until date of auction. **Protections for High-Cost Mortgages:** Georgia Fair Lending Act, Ga. Code Ann. § 7-6A-1 to 7-6A-11 **Redemption Period:** None. **Eviction Process:** New owner may seek immediate order to evict former owners after sale. **Deficiency Judgments:** Not allowed, unless court confirms property was auctioned at fair market value. **Limits on Deficiency Judgments:** Sale will not be confirmed unless court is satisfied the sales price was for the true market value of the house. No deficiency is allowed unless the bank makes a request to the court and the sale is confirmed. **Cash Exempted in Bankruptcy:** $5,600 for single person, $11,200 for married couple. **State Statutes:** Ga. Code Ann. § 44-14-160 to 44-14-191.

Hawaii Foreclosure Laws

Expected Timeline: Three to four months **Security Instrument:** Mortgage **Type of Process:** About half are judicial, other half are non judicial **Protections for Service members:** Haw. Rev. Stat. § 657D-1 to 657D-63 **Time to Respond:** Twenty to thirty days to respond after foreclosure lawsuit is filed in judicial proceedings. In Non judicial, lender must publish notice in newspaper for three consecutive weeks. The last notice must be fourteen days before the sale. Notice posted on property must be done 21 days before sale. Alternatively, federally insured lending institutions can give homeowners a 60-day notice of default. **Reinstatement Period:** Allowed up to 60 days after notice of default in non judicial foreclosure, or up to three days before sale in alternate notification process. **Protections for High-Cost Mortgages:** None. **Redemption Period:** None. **Eviction Process:** New owner must be granted court order to evict former owners. **Deficiency Judgments:** Allowed, but must be requested in original foreclosure lawsuit complaint. **Limits on Deficiency Judgments:** Allowed in some types of foreclosure, not allowed in others. **Cash Exempted in Bankruptcy:** $11,000 for single person, $22,000 for married couples. **State Statutes:** Haw. Rev. Stat. § 667-1 to 667-46.

Idaho Foreclosure Laws

Expected Timeline: Five to six months **Security Instrument:** Deed of trust **Type of Process:** Non judicial **Protections for Service members:** Idaho Code § 46-409 **Time to Respond:** Homeowners must be given 120-day Notice of Default and Sale. Personal service must be attempted and notice posted on property at least 30 days before sale. Newspaper publication notices required over four consecutive weeks at least 30 before auction date. **Reinstatement Period:** Available within 115 days of Notice of Default and Sale being filed. **Protections for High-Cost Mortgages:** None. **Redemption Period:** None. **Eviction Process:** New owner entitled to possession ten days after sale. Court order required to remove former owners from property. Eviction hearing must be scheduled within twelve days of a complaint and summons being filed in court. **Deficiency Judgments:** May be allowed if separate lawsuit is brought within three months of sale. Amount of judgment restricted to fair market value at time of sale. **Limits on Deficiency Judgments:** Lawsuit for deficiency must be brought within 3 months of the public auction. Deficiency limited by fair market value as of the date of the sale. **Cash Exempted in Bankruptcy:** None. **State Statutes:** Idaho Code § 45-1505 to 45-1515.

Illinois Foreclosure Laws

Expected Timeline: Seven to ten months **Security Instrument:** Mortgage **Type of Process:** Judicial **Protections for Service members:** 330 Ill. Comp. Stat. § 60/5.1 **Time to Respond:** Homeowners have 20-30 days to respond after being served with the foreclosure lawsuit. If judgment is awarded to lender, notice of sale must be published between 45 and 7 days before auction date. **Reinstatement Period:** Lenders must inform homeowners of right to reinstate at least 30 days before filing lawsuit. Homeowners have 90 days to reinstate loan. See High-Risk Home Loan Act. **Protections for High-Cost Mortgages:** High-Risk Home Loan Act, 815 Ill. COmp. Stat. § 137/1 to 137/175 **Redemption Period:** Seven months after complaint served or three months after foreclosure judgment entered -- whichever is later. **Eviction Process:** Court may order eviction within 30 days of sale, although new owner must file complaint for forcible entry and detainer in order to evict anyone not personally served in foreclosure lawsuit. 735 Ill. Comp. Stat. § 735, ILCS 5/9-101, 735 ILCS 5/15-1508(g). **Deficiency Judgments:** Allowed, but must be requested as part of initial foreclosure lawsuit. **Limits on Deficiency Judgments:** Deficiency judgments are allowed. **Cash Exempted in Bankruptcy:** $4,000 for single person, $8,000 for married couple. **State Statutes:** 735 Ill. Comp. Stat. § 5/15-1501 to 5/15-1512.

Indiana Foreclosure Laws

Expected Timeline: Five to seven months **Security Instrument:** Mortgage **Type of Process:** Judicial **Protections for Service members:** None. **Time to Respond:** Homeowners have 30 days before filing complaint in court for foreclosure. Notice must be personally served and after complaint is filed, property may not be sold for three months. Notice of sale must be published for three consecutive weeks beginning at least 30 days before action is commenced. **Reinstatement Period:** Available for high cost loans anytime before sale. **Protections for High-Cost Mortgages:** Ind. Code § 24-9-5-1 **Redemption Period:** None. **Eviction Process:** Former owners must be given five-day notice to quit. After that, new owner may request possession from court. **Deficiency Judgments:** Allowed if authorized by loan documents and if borrowers do not waive applicable waiting period. **Limits on Deficiency Judgments:** If there is an agreement and an applicable waiting period is not waived, a deficiency judgment may be obtained. **Cash Exempted in Bankruptcy:** $300 for single person, $600 for married couples. **State Statutes:** Ind Code § 32-30-10-1 to 32-30-10-14, 32-29-1-1 to 32-39-1-11, 32-29-7-1 to 32-29-7-14.

Iowa Foreclosure Laws

Expected Timeline: Five to six months **Security Instrument:** Mortgage **Type of Process:** Most often judicial. Lenders may use non judicial if homeowners agree to give up possession of property and lender agrees not to pursue deficiency judgment. **Protections for Service members:** Iowa Code § 29A.102 **Time to Respond:** Homeowners must be mailed notice of default and right to cure at least 30 days before foreclosure lawsuit is filed. Notice must be published and posted four weeks before filing. **Reinstatement Period:** Allowed within 30 days of homeowners receiving notice of default. **Protections for High-Cost Mortgages:** None. **Redemption Period:** One year after sheriff sale. **Eviction Process:** New owner must file forcible entry and detainer lawsuit in order to evict. Hearing will be held within seven days, but former owner must be personally served with notice not less than three days before hearing. **Deficiency Judgments:** Allowed. **Limits on Deficiency Judgments:** Deficiency not allowed if non judicial foreclosure process is used. Otherwise, deficiencies may be limited by statute. **Cash Exempted in Bankruptcy:** $100 for single person, $200 for married couple. **State Statutes:** Iowa Code § 654.1 to 654.26.

Kansas Foreclosure Laws

Expected Timeline: About four months **Security Instrument:** Mortgage **Type of Process:** Judicial **Protections for Service members:** None. **Time to Respond:** Twenty days to respond to foreclosure lawsuit with personal service. Forty-one days to respond to lawsuit if notice is only published. Notice of sale must be published at least three times before auction date, the last time of which must be between 7 and 14 days before sale. **Reinstatement Period:** None. **Protections for High-Cost Mortgages:** None. **Redemption Period:** Depends on how much principal was paid on loan. If more than one-third was paid off, redemption is twelve months from date of sale. If less than one-third, redemption is three months. **Eviction Process:** New owner must file petition in court for ejectment of former owners. Eviction order can come within a week or two. **Deficiency Judgments:** Allowed if property sold at auction for fair market value. **Limits on Deficiency Judgments:** Deficiencies are allowed, but the court can refuse to allow confirmation of the sale or set an upset price. **Cash Exempted in Bankruptcy:** None. **State Statutes:** Kan. Stat. Ann. § 60-2410.

Kentucky Foreclosure Laws

Expected Timeline: Five to six months **Security Instrument:** Mortgage **Type of Process:** Judicial **Protections for Service members:** Ky. Rev. Stat. Ann. § 38-510 **Time to Respond:** Twenty days to respond after being served with foreclosure complaint. Notice of sale must be posted on courthouse door or published for three weeks at least fifteen days before scheduled auction. **Reinstatement Period:** Notice of right to reinstatement must be served at least 30 days before filing lawsuit, if the loan is a high-interest loan. See Ky. Rev. Stat. Ann. § 360.100 **Protections for High-Cost Mortgages:** Ky. Rev. Stat. Ann. § 360-100 **Redemption Period:** If property sells for less than two-thirds of appraised value, redemption is one year after sale. **Eviction Process:** Immediate writ of possession may be granted by court. **Deficiency Judgments:** Allowed if homeowner is personally served with complaint or fails to respond to complaint. **Limits on Deficiency Judgments:** Deficiency allowed if homeowners fail to answer foreclosure lawsuit or if they are served with the paperwork in-hand. **Cash Exempted in Bankruptcy:** $1,000 for single person, $2,000 for married couple. **State Statutes:** Ky. Rev. Stat. Ann. § 426.525 to 426.720.

Louisiana Foreclosure Laws

Expected Timeline: Two to six months **Security Instrument:** Mortgage **Type of Process:** Judicial "executory" proceeding **Protections for Service members:** La. Rev. Stat. Ann § 29:315 **Time to Respond:** Noice of sale is part of petition posted on property. **Reinstatement Period:** None. **Protections for High-Cost Mortgages:** None. **Redemption Period:** None. **Eviction Process:** Sheriff may seize property without notice after court grants writ of seizure and sale. **Deficiency Judgments:** Allowed. **Limits on Deficiency Judgments:** Deficiency only allowed in ordinary proceeding or executory proceeding if property has had an appraisal done under the state regulations. **Cash Exempted in Bankruptcy:** None. **State Statutes:** La. Code Civ. Proc. Ann. Arts. 3721 to 3753, 2631 to 2772.

Maine Foreclosure Laws

Expected Timeline: Six to ten months **Security Instrument:** Mortgage **Type of Process:** Judicial **Protections for Service members:** Me. Rev. Stat. Ann. titl 37-B, § 387 **Time to Respond:** Twenty to thirty days to respond to foreclosure lawsuit. If judgment is awarded to bank, notice must be published within 90 days after redemption period expires. Notice must be published for three consecutive weeks, and sale will be held 30-45 days after first publication. Notice of sale must be mailed to owners at least 30 days before sale. **Reinstatement Period:** Homeowners may receive two months to reinstate, with a two-month extension possible. Lender may allow owners to reinstate at any time before sale. **Protections for High-Cost Mortgages:** None. **Redemption Period:** Ninety days from date of judgment, unless homeowners appeal. **Eviction Process:** No specific timeline for eviction. New owner will go to court to get eviction order, and eviction can take from two weeks to a month. Longer period will result if former owners respond to complaint. **Deficiency Judgments:** Allowed. **Limits on Deficiency Judgments:** Deficiencies are limited to an amount set on the date of the sale. If the bank that owns the mortgage is the high bidder at auction, any deficiency is also limited to the fair market value of the property. **Cash Exempted in Bankruptcy:** $6,400 for single person, $12,800 for married couples. **State Statutes:** Me. Rev. Stat. Ann. tit. 14, § 6101 to 6325.

Maryland Foreclosure Laws

Expected Timeline: About two months **Security Instrument:** Mortgage or Deed of Trust **Type of Process:** Judicial or Non judicial **Protections for Service members:** Md. Code Ann. [Pub. Safety] § 13-705 **Time to Respond:** Lender not required to notify borrower of lawsuit. Notice of intent to foreclose must be sent to homeowners within 45 days before sheriff sale. Notice must be by first class/certified mail with return receipt requested. Notice must also be published for three consecutive weeks. Notice must be served on homeowners at least 10 but not more than 30 days before auction. **Reinstatement Period:** Allowed until one day before sale. **Protections for High-Cost Mortgages:** None. **Redemption Period:** Homeowners may request redemption from court. **Eviction Process:** No specific timelines for eviction. New owner will go to court to get order and process can take two weeks to a month. Longer process may be a result of homeowners answering complaint. **Deficiency Judgments:**

Allowed, if foreclosing party requests it of supervising court after sale. **Limits on Deficiency Judgments:** Report of sale and audit are required, but a deficiency can be obtained by filing a motion in court after the sale has been conducted. **Cash Exempted in Bankruptcy:** $6,000 for single person, $12,000 for married couple. **State Statutes:** Md. Code Ann. [Real Property] § 7-105.

Massachusetts Foreclosure Laws

Expected Timeline: Three to four months **Security Instrument:** Mortgage **Type of Process:** Most commonly non judicial, but judicial also available. **Protections for Service members:** None. **Time to Respond:** Homeowners must receive notice of sale at least 14 days before scheduled sheriff sale date. Notice must be published for three consecutive weeks before auction. **Reinstatement Period:** In the case of a conditional judgment, homeowners have two months to reinstate the loan. Homeowners are entitled to a 90 day notice of right to reinstate before acceleration of mortgage can occur. Notice must be served by first class mail **Protections for High-Cost Mortgages:** Predatory Home Loan Practices Act, Mass. Gen. Laws ch. 183C, § 1-19 **Redemption Period:** None. **Eviction Process:** If conditional judgment is awarded to lender, new owner can use writ of possession to evict former owners without notice once reinstatement period has expired. **Deficiency Judgments:** Allowed, must be brought as separate lawsuit if a notice of intent to seek a deficiency is included in notice of sale. Notice of sale must be mailed to homeowners at least 21 days before auction date. **Limits on Deficiency Judgments:** If a deficiency is to be pursued, the bank must include a notice of intent to seek deficiency with the required Notice of Sale. This Notice of Sale must be served on the borrowers at least 21 days prior to the actual auction. **Cash Exempted in Bankruptcy:** $11,000 for single person, $22,000 for married couple. **State Statutes:** Mass. Gen. Laws ch. 244, § 14.

Michigan Foreclosure Laws

Expected Timeline: About two months. **Security Instrument:** Mortgage or Deed of Trust **Type of Process:** Judicial or Non judicial **Protections for Service members:** Mich. COmp. Laws § 32.517 **Time to Respond:** Homeowners do not need to receive notice via mail. Notice required to be published for four consecutive weeks before sheriff sale. Notice must also be published on property within 15 days of first publication. **Reinstatement Period:** Reinstatement is allowed any time before the sale in judicial foreclosure. There is no reinstatement in non judicial foreclosure. **Protections for High-Cost Mortgages:** None. **Redemption Period:** For owner-occupied properties owing more than two-thirds of principal, redemption is six months after sheriff sale. For properties owing less than two-thirds, redemption is one year. For abandoned properties that owe at least two-thirds, redemption period is between one and three months. **Eviction Process:** In judicial foreclosure, the judge may order eviction once the redemption period has ended. In non judicial foreclosure, the new owner will go to court to seek order for eviction, which may take from two weeks to a month. **Deficiency Judgments:** Allowed in either judicial or non judicial foreclosure. **Limits on Deficiency Judgments:** If the mortgagee bank purchases the property at auction, homeowners may use as a defense that the sale price was for less than the fair market value of the property. **Cash Exempted in Bankruptcy:** $11,000 for single person, $22,000 for married couple. **State Statutes:** Mich. Comp. Laws § 600.3101 to 600.3180, 600.3201 to 600.3280.

Minnesota Foreclosure Laws

Expected Timeline: Two to three months **Security Instrument:** Mortgage or Deed of Trust **Type of Process:** Judicial or non judicial **Protections for Service members:** Minn. Stat. § 72A.20(8)(b),(c) **Time to Respond:** Notice of sale must be published six weeks before scheduled sheriff sale. Notice must also be served on homeowners at least four weeks before auction date. **Reinstatement Period:** Loan may be reinstated any time before auction. **Protections for High-Cost Mortgages:** None. **Redemption Period:** Former owners may stay in property and redeem for six months after sheriff sale. **Eviction Process:** One month after eviction ends, new owner may give one month's notice. Then an eviction lawsuit may be filed. **Deficiency Judgments:** Deficiency judgments are not available in non judicial foreclosure with a six month redemption period. **Limits on Deficiency Judgments:** Deficiency allowed, but limited by fair market value determined through a jury trial. If non judicial foreclosure is used and the six-month redemption period is available, no deficiency is allowed. **Cash Exempted in Bankruptcy:** $11,000 for single person, $22,000 for married couple. **State Statutes:** Minn. Stat. § 580.01 to 580.30.

Mississippi Foreclosure Laws

Expected Timeline: Two to three months **Security Instrument:** Mortgage or Deed of Trust. Deed of trust is more likely in Mississippi foreclosures. **Type of Process:** Judicial or Non judicial. Non judicial foreclosure will be used most frequently. **Protections for Service members:** Miss. Code Ann. § 74-25-5(2)(m) **Time to Respond:** Notice does not need to be sent to homeowners, but does need to be published three consecutive weeks before sheriff sale. **Reinstatement Period:** Loan may be reinstated any time until sale date. **Protections for High-Cost Mortgages:** None. **Redemption Period:** None. **Eviction Process:** New owner will have to initiate lawsuit for eviction. This may take two weeks to a month, depending on if former owners respond to lawsuit or not. **Deficiency Judgments:** Allowed if separate lawsuit is filed within one year of auction. Deficiency may not be allowed if buyer at auction is original lender and house sold for less than fair market value. **Limits on Deficiency Judgments:** Judgment allowed if suit filed within one year of the auction. If the mortgagee bank was the winner at auction, deficiency may be denied based on unreasonably low sales price. **Cash Exempted in Bankruptcy:** None. **State Statutes:** Miss. Code Ann. § 89-1-55 to 89-1-59.

Missouri Foreclosure Laws

Expected Timeline: About two months **Security Instrument:** Mortgage or Deed of Trust. Deed of trust most common. **Type of Process:** Judicial or Non judicial. Non judicial foreclosure most common in Missouri. **Protections for Service members:** Mo. Ann. Stat. § 41.944 **Time to Respond:** Twenty day notice of sale must be sent by registered and certified mail to homeowners. **Reinstatement Period:** None. **Protections for High-Cost Mortgages:** None. **Redemption Period:** Homeowners must give foreclosing party a ten-day notice of intent to redeem before the sheriff sale. The lender must buy the property at the auction. If these conditions are met, redemption is available up to one year after sale. **Eviction Process:** New owner must give former owners one month's written notice to vacate the property. **Deficiency Judgments:** Allowed in separate lawsuit. **Limits on Deficiency Judgments:** Deficiency judgments allowed. **Cash Exempted in Bankruptcy:** $600 for single person, $1,200 for married couple. **State Statutes:** Mo. Rev. Stat. § 443.290 to 443.453.

Montana Foreclosure Laws

Expected Timeline: About five months **Security Instrument:** Mortgage or Deed of Trust. Most single family properties secured with deed of trust. **Type of Process:** Judicial or Non judicial. Non judicial most commonly used in foreclosures. **Protections for Service members:** Mont. Code. Ann. § 10-1-903 **Time to Respond:** Lender must give homeowners a thirty day notice before sheriff sale. **Reinstatement Period:** None. **Protections for High-Cost Mortgages:** None. **Redemption Period:** Redemption is allowed within one year of foreclosure auction. **Eviction Process:** Must be initiated by lawsuit after redemption period has expired. **Deficiency Judgments:** Allowed in judicial foreclosures. **Limits on Deficiency Judgments:** Allowed on a purchase money mortgage only under judicial foreclosure procedures. **Cash Exempted in Bankruptcy:** None. **State Statutes:** Mont. Code Ann. § 71-1-222 to 71-1-235, 71-1-301 to 71-1-321.

Nebraska Foreclosure Laws

Expected Timeline: Five to six months **Security Instrument:** Mortgage **Type of Process:** Judicial **Protections for Service members:** None. **Time to Respond:** After judgment has been entered in foreclosure lawsuit, lender must post notice of sale on courthouse door. Notice must also be posted in five other public places and published for four weeks before sheriff sale. **Reinstatement Period:** Available while lawsuit is proceeding and before the sale. **Protections for High-Cost Mortgages:** None. **Redemption Period:** None. **Eviction Process:** Court may order former owners to leave property after sheriff sale. **Deficiency Judgments:** Allowed if brought in a separate lawsuit. **Limits on Deficiency Judgments:** Suit must be brought within 3 months of auction date. A deficiency is limited to the lessor of the difference between the amount owed to the bank and the fair market value at the time of the sale, or the difference between the amount owed and the sales price at auction. **Cash Exempted in Bankruptcy:** $2,500 for single person, $5,000 for married couple. **State Statutes:** Neb. Rev. Stat. § 25-2137 to 25-2155.

Nevada Foreclosure Laws

Expected Timeline: About four months **Security Instrument:** Mortgage or Deed of Trust. Deed of trust most common. **Type of Process:** Judicial or Non judicial. Non judicial foreclosure most common in Nevada. **Protections for Service members:** None. **Time to Respond:** Homeowners must receive two notices. The first is a three month Notice of Default and Election to sell. The second is a three week notice of sale. **Reinstatement Period:** Homeowners may reinstate the loan within 35 days of lender filing notice of default with recorder's office. **Protections for High-Cost Mortgages:** Nev. Rev. Stat. § 598D.010 to 598D.150 **Redemption Period:** None. **Eviction Process:** New owner must give former owners a three day notice to quit the property. After this has expired, an eviction lawsuit may be filed. **Deficiency Judgments:** Allowed if a separate lawsuit is filed within six months of sheriff sale. Certain limits apply. **Limits on Deficiency Judgments:** Allowed, but limited to the lessor of the following: the difference between the debt and the fair market value; or the difference between the debt and the sales price at auction, including interest from the date of sale. **Cash Exempted in Bankruptcy:** None. **State Statutes:** Nev. Rev. Stat. § 107.080.

New Hampshire Foreclosure Laws

Expected Timeline: Two to three months **Security Instrument:** Mortgage or Deed of Trust. Mortgages most common. **Type of Process:** Judicial or Non judicial. Judicial foreclosure most common. **Protections for Service members:** N.H. Rev. Stat. Ann. § 540-11-a **Time to Respond:** Lender must file lawsuit in court, then obtain a Decree of Sale. Court gives homeowners a set period of time to pay delinquent amount of loan plus costs. **Reinstatement Period:** None in Non judicial foreclosure. **Protections for High-Cost Mortgages:** None. **Redemption Period:** None. **Eviction Process:** Former owners must be given a thirty day notice to quit property. After this expires, new owner may bring eviction lawsuit. Former owners have seven days to respond to lawsuit. **Deficiency Judgments:** Allowed if brought in separate lawsuit after sheriff sale. **Limits on Deficiency Judgments:** Allowed if action is brought in court after sale. **Cash Exempted in Bankruptcy:** $11,000 for single person, $22,000 for married couple. **State Statutes:** N.H. Rev. Stat. Ann. § 479.25.

New Jersey Foreclosure Laws

Expected Timeline: Three to ten months **Security Instrument:** Mortgage **Type of Process:** Judicial **Protections for Service members:** N.J. Stat. Ann. § 38:23C-1 to 38:23C-26 **Time to Respond:** Lender must send notice to homeowners via registered or certified mail with return receipt requested at least thirty days before filing lawsuit. Notice must be posted on property two times in four weeks before suit or published in two newspapers. Notice must also be sent to mortgagor and other parties. **Reinstatement Period:** Up to date of final judgment in lawsuit. **Protections for High-Cost Mortgages:** Home Ownership Security Act, N.J. Stat. Ann. § 46:10B-22 to 10B-35 **Redemption Period:** Redemption period is six months from date final judgment is entered in lawsuit. **Eviction Process:** Former owners do not have to be served with notice to leave property after sheriff sale. **Deficiency Judgments:** Allowed if brought in separate lawsuit within three months after sheriff sale. Amount of judgment is restricted to difference between fair market value and loan. **Limits on Deficiency Judgments:** Judgment allowed only on the note after foreclosure, but no personal deficiency judgment allowed. Deficiency is limited by the fair market value of the property, and action must be brought into court within 3 months of sale. **Cash Exempted in Bankruptcy:** $11,000 for single person, $22,000 for married couple. **State Statutes:** N.J. Stat. Ann. § 2A:50-1 to 2A:50-21, 2A:50-56 to 2A:50-58.

New Mexico Foreclosure Laws

Expected Timeline: Four to six months **Security Instrument:** Mortgage **Type of Process:** Judicial **Protections for Service members:** N.M. Stat. Ann. § 20-4-7.1 **Time to Respond:** Twenty to thirty days to respond to foreclosure lawsuit. Sheriff sale may not be scheduled for at least 30 days after final judgment in case. Notice must be published for four consecutive weeks and posted in six public places throughout county. **Reinstatement Period:** Homeowners have thirty day right to reinstate if they have a high cost loan. **Protections for High-Cost Mortgages:** Home Loan Protection Act, N.M. Stat. Ann. § 58-21A-1 to 58-21A-14 **Redemption Period:** Redemption period is nine months after sheriff sale. **Eviction Process:** Former owners must be given a three day notice to quit the property. After this, the new owner may file an eviction lawsuit. Former owners have three to seven days to respond to lawsuit. **Deficiency Judgments:** Allowed if brought in a separate lawsuit. Deficiency may not be recovered from low income households. **Limits on Deficiency Judgments:** Allowed in judicial foreclosure, but property cannot be sold for less than 2/3 of its appraised value. In Non judicial foreclosure, creditor can sue for deficiency within 6 years of sale, unless property was occupied by a low-income household. **Cash Exempted in Bankruptcy:** $11,000 for single person, $22,000 for married couple. **State Statutes:** N.M. Stat. Ann. § 48-7-1 to 48-7-24, 39-5-1 to 35-5-23.

New York Foreclosure Laws

Expected Timeline: Four to eight months **Security Instrument:** Mortgage **Type of Process:** Judicial **Protections for Service members:** N.Y. Mil. Law § 308 **Time to Respond:** Lenders must send a pre-foreclosure notice to borrowers at least 90 days before beginning foreclosure proceedings. Homeowners have twenty to thirty days to respond to the foreclosure lawsuit. **Reinstatement Period:** Loan may be reinstated any time before final judgment is entered in case. **Protections for High-Cost Mortgages:** N.Y. Banking Law § 6-1, Real Property Law § 265-a (Home Equity Theft Prevention Act) **Redemption Period:** None. **Eviction Process:** Former owners must receive seven day notice to quit property. After this, new owner may request court for possession. Court petition must be served on former owners five to twelve days before court hearing. **Deficiency Judgments:** Allowed if homeowners are personally served in lawsuit or appear at lawsuit. Amount of deficiency limited to debt less fair market value or sales price (whichever is higher). **Limits on Deficiency Judgments:** Deficiencies limited by fair market value of property, and are only allowed if homeowner was served in-hand or appeared for lawsuit. **Cash Exempted in Bankruptcy:** $2,500 for single person, $5,000 for married couple. **State Statutes:** N.Y. Real Prop. Act. Law § 1301-1391.

North Carolina Foreclosure Laws

Expected Timeline: Two to four months **Security Instrument:** Mortgage or Deed of Trust. Deed of trust most common. **Type of Process:** Judicial or Non judicial. Non judicial foreclosure are most common. **Protections for Service members:** None. **Time to Respond:** Notice of default must be given to homeowners thirty days before notice of hearing. Notice of hearing must be given at least ten days before hearing. Twenty day notice of sale must be given if sale is posted and published, or else ten day notice of sale if homeowners are served by mail. **Reinstatement Period:** None. **Protections for High-Cost Mortgages:** North Carolina High Cost Mortgage Act, N.C. Gen. Stat. § 24-1.1E **Redemption Period:** Redemption period is ten days after sheriff sale date. **Eviction Process:** Former owners must be given a ten day notice to quit property. After this, new owner may go to court for writ of possession and summary eviction. **Deficiency Judgments:** Not allowed in Non judicial foreclosures. **Limits on Deficiency Judgments:** May be limited by fair market value in judicial cases. No deficiency allowed in Non judicial foreclosure of purchase money mortgage. **Cash Exempted in Bankruptcy:** $5,500 for single person, $11,000 for married couple. **State Statutes:** N.C. Gen. Stat. § 45-1.1 to 45-21.33.

North Dakota Foreclosure Laws

Expected Timeline: Three to five months **Security Instrument:** Mortgage **Type of Process:** Judicial **Protections for Service members:** None. **Time to Respond:** Homeowners must be served with a notice of intent to foreclose 30 to 90 days before filing a foreclosure lawsuit. The time to respond to the lawsuit is twenty to thirty days. **Reinstatement Period:** Homeowners may reinstate the loan any time up to thirty days after being served with a notice of intent to foreclose. **Protections for High-Cost Mortgages:** None. **Redemption Period:** Redemption period is sixty days after the sheriff sale. **Eviction Process:** Sheriff may evict former owners immediately upon expiration of redemption period. **Deficiency Judgments:** Not allowed. **Limits on Deficiency Judgments:** Deficiencies limited by fair market value or appraised value, but allowed on land of more than 40 acres. Not allowed on residential property of four or fewer units on less 40 acres. **Cash Exempted in Bankruptcy:** $7,500 for single person, $15,000 for married couple. **State Statutes:** N.D. Cent. Code § 32-19-01 to 32-19-41.

Ohio Foreclosure Laws

Expected Timeline: Five to seven months **Security Instrument:** Mortgage **Type of Process:** Judicial **Protections for Service members:** Ohio Rev. Code Ann. § 5919.29, 5923.12 **Time to Respond:** Homeowners have twenty to thirty days to respond to the foreclosure lawsuit. After judgment has been entered for foreclosure, homeowners must be served with a seven day notice of sale. Notice of sale must be published within 30 days of sale date. **Reinstatement Period:** None. **Protections for High-Cost Mortgages:** None. **Redemption Period:** Redemption period lasts until court confirms sheriff sale. **Eviction Process:** New owner will have to initiate lawsuit in court for eviction order. This process may take between two weeks and a month, depending on if homeowners respond to complaint. **Deficiency Judgments:**

Allowed. **Limits on Deficiency Judgments:** Allowed but void after two years after sale date. The property cannot be sold for less than 2/3 of its appraised market value. **Cash Exempted in Bankruptcy:** $400 for single person, $800 for married couple. **State Statutes:** Ohio Rev. Code Ann. § 2323.07, 2329.26, 5721.38.

Oklahoma Foreclosure Laws

Expected Timeline: Four to seven months **Security Instrument:** Mortgage or Deed of Trust. Most common is mortgage. **Type of Process:** Judicial or Non judicial. Judicial foreclosure most commonly used. **Protections for Service members:** Okla. Stat. titl 44, § 208.1 **Time to Respond:** Homeowners have twenty to thirty days to respond to foreclosure lawsuit. Notice of sale must be served at least ten days before sale if by mail. If served by publication, publishing must start at least thirty days before sale. If Non judicial foreclosure is used, homeowners must receive a 35 day notice of intent to foreclose and a 30 day notice of sale. **Reinstatement Period:** In Non judicial foreclosure, homeowners may reinstate within 35 days of service of notice of intent to foreclose. **Protections for High-Cost Mortgages:** None. **Redemption Period:** Redemption period lasts until sheriff sale is confirmed by court. **Eviction Process:** Immediate possession may be granted to new owner by judge. Failure to leave property may be considered contempt of court. **Deficiency Judgments:** Allowed if requested within 90 days of sheriff sale. The amount of a deficiency is limited by fair market value. **Limits on Deficiency Judgments:** Limited by fair market value as of auction date. Objections may be filed to confirmation of sale. **Cash Exempted in Bankruptcy:** None. **State Statutes:** Okla. Stat. tit. 12, § 686, 764 to 765, 773, Okla. Stat. tit. 46, § 41 to 49.

Oregon Foreclosure Laws

Expected Timeline: About five months **Security Instrument:** Mortgage and Deed of Trust. Deed of trust most common. **Type of Process:** Judicial and Non judicial. Non judicial foreclosure most commonly used. **Protections for Service members:** Or. Rev. Stat. § 105.111 **Time to Respond:** Notice of default must be served by mail. Notice of sale must be sent at least 120 days before sheriff sale. If judicial foreclosure is used, homeowners have twenty to thirty days to respond to complaint. **Reinstatement Period:** Homeowners may reinstate loan up to five days before sale. **Protections for High-Cost Mortgages:** None. **Redemption Period:** None. **Eviction Process:** New owner may take possession ten days after sheriff sale. Former owners can be evicted with no notice. **Deficiency Judgments:** Not allowed under Oregon foreclosure law. **Limits on Deficiency Judgments:** Deficiency judgments not allowed on judicial foreclosure proceedings involving residential mortgages, or in Non judicial foreclosures. **Cash Exempted in Bankruptcy:** $7,500 for single person, $15,000 for married couple. **State Statutes:** Or. Rev. Stat. § 86.735 to 86.795, 88.080-88.100.

Pennsylvania Foreclosure Laws

Expected Timeline: Three to nine months **Security Instrument:** Mortgage **Type of Process:** Judicial **Protections for Service members:** Pa. Stat. Ann. tit. 51, § 4105 **Time to Respond:** Homeowners must be served with thirty day notice of intention to foreclose. Notice must be sent certified mail. Homeowners have twenty to thirty days to respond to lawsuit. **Reinstatement Period:** Homeowners may reinstate up to one hour before bidding starts at sheriff sale. **Protections for High-Cost Mortgages:** None. **Redemption Period:** None. **Eviction Process:** No specific eviction timeline under PA foreclosure laws. New owner will go to court for eviction order. Process may take two weeks to a month, depending on if homeowners respond to lawsuit or not. **Deficiency Judgments:** Allowed if brought in separate lawsuit after sheriff sale. **Limits on Deficiency Judgments:** Allowed if a separate action is filed in court after auction. If the mortgagee purchases the property at auction, any deficiency is limited by the fair market value. **Cash Exempted in Bankruptcy:** $11,000 for single person, $22,000 for married couple. **State Statutes:** Pa. Stat. Ann. tit. 35, § 1680.402c to 1680.409c, Pa. Stat. Ann. tit. 41, § 403 to 404, Pa. R. Civ. P. 1141-1150.

Rhode Island Foreclosure Laws

Expected Timeline: Two to three months **Security Instrument:** Mortgage with a power of sale clause **Type of Process:** Judicial or Non judicial. Non judicial most common type of foreclosure. **Protections for Service members:** R.I. Gen Laws § 30-7-10 **Time to Respond:** Notice of sale must be published for three consecutive weeks before sheriff sale. The first publication must be at least 21 days before auction. Notice of sale must be served on homeowners by mail at least thirty days before first publication of sale. **Reinstatement Period: None. Protections for High-Cost Mortgages:** Rhode Island Home Loan Protection Act, R.I. Gen. Laws § 35-25.2-1 to 35-25.2-11 **Redemption Period:** Former owner must file lawsuit for redemption period. Redemption may be allowed up to three years after sheriff sale. **Eviction Process:** New owner must give twenty day notice to quit property. After that, new owner may go to court for summary eviction. This process may take between two weeks and a month, depending on if former owners answer lawsuit or not. **Deficiency Judgments:** Allowed if brought in separate lawsuit after foreclosure auction. **Limits on Deficiency Judgments:** Deficiency judgments are allowed. **Cash Exempted in Bankruptcy:** $11,000 for single person, $22,000 for married couple. **State Statutes:** R.I. Gen. Laws § 34-27-1 to 34-27-5.

South Carolina Foreclosure Laws

Expected Timeline: About six months **Security Instrument:** Mortgage **Type of Process:** Judicial **Protections for Service members:** None. **Time to Respond:** Homeowners have twenty to thirty days to respond to foreclosure lawsuit. Notice of sale must be published three weeks before sheriff sale. Notice must also be posted in three public places. **Reinstatement Period: None. Protections for High-Cost Mortgages:** South Carolina High-Cost and Consumer Home Loans Act, S.C. Code Ann. § 37-23-10 to 37-23-85 **Redemption Period:** None. **Eviction Process:** New owner must give a ten day notice of termination. **Deficiency Judgments:** Allowed as part of initial foreclosure lawsuit. **Limits on Deficiency Judgments:** Homeowners may request court to issue an order of appraisal within 30 days of the auction. If this is done, deficiency is limited by the amount of the debt over the appraised value. **Cash Exempted in Bankruptcy:** $5,000 for single person, $10,000 for married couple. **State Statutes:** S.C. Code Ann. § 15-39-610, 29-3-630 to 29-3-790.

South Dakota Foreclosure Laws

Expected Timeline: Six to nine months **Security Instrument:** Mortgage or Deed of Trust. Mortgages most commonly used. **Type of Process:** Judicial or

Non judicial. Non judicial foreclosure most common. **Protections for Service members:** S.D. Cod. Laws Ann. § 33-17-15.1 **Time to Respond:** In Non judicial foreclosure, notice must be published for four weeks. Notice must also be given to homeowners at least 21 days before sheriff sale. **Reinstatement Period:** Reinstatement is available under judicial foreclosure until court enters final judgment. **Protections for High-Cost Mortgages:** None. **Redemption Period:** Redemption is allowed for one year after date of foreclosure auction. This may not apply if mortgage is designated as a short-term redemption mortgage in loan documents. In this case, redemption is six months from date of sheriff sale. **Eviction Process:** In a judicial foreclosure, the judge may order possession given to new owner after redemption ends. Former owners must receive a three day notice to quit. After this, the new owner may file an eviction lawsuit. **Deficiency Judgments:** Allowed. If lender buys property back at auction, deficiency amount is limited to difference between fair market value at time of sale and balance due on mortgage. **Limits on Deficiency Judgments:** If mortgagee or holder of note purchases the property at auction, any deficiency is limited by the market value. In judicial foreclosure proceedings, a deficiency judgment may be barred. In cases of voluntary foreclosure, no deficiency or surplus is allowed. **Cash Exempted in Bankruptcy:** $4,000 for single person, $6,000 for married couple. **State Statutes:** S.D. Cod. Laws Ann. § 21-48-1 to 21-48-26.

Tennessee Foreclosure Laws

Expected Timeline: About two months **Security Instrument:** Mortgage or Deed of Trust. Deed of trust most common. **Type of Process:** Judicial or Non judicial. Non judicial foreclosure most commonly used. **Protections for Service members:** Tenn. Code Ann. § 26-1-111 **Time to Respond:** Notice must be published twenty days before sale or posted thirty days before sale. Notice must be sent to homeowners via registered mail before first publication of sheriff sale. **Reinstatement Period:** None. **Protections for High-Cost Mortgages:** None. **Redemption Period:** There is a two year redemption period if judicial foreclosure is used unless waived in mortgage documents. **Eviction Process:** New owner may file forcible entry and detainer lawsuit. Warrant must be served on former owner with a trial six days after service. AN immediate writ of possession will order the sheriff to evict. **Deficiency Judgments:** Allowed. **Limits on Deficiency Judgments:** Deficiency judgments are allowed. **Cash Exempted in Bankruptcy:** $4,000 for single person, $8,000 for married couple. **State Statutes:** Tenn. Code Ann. § 35-5-101 to 35-5-111, 66-8-101 to 66-8-102.

Texas Foreclosure Laws

Expected Timeline: About two months **Security Instrument:** Mortgage or Deed of Trust. Deed of trust most common. **Type of Process:** Judicial or Non judicial. Non judicial foreclosure used most often. **Protections for Service members:** Tex. Civ. Prac. & Rem. Code § 16.022 **Time to Respond:** Notice of default must be served twenty days before serving notice of sale. Notice of sale must be served at least 21 days before sale. Notice must also be posted on courthouse. **Reinstatement Period:** Notice of default must be served twenty days before serving notice of sale. Notice of sale must be served at least 21 days before sale. Notice must also be posted on courthouse. **Protections for High-Cost Mortgages:** None. **Redemption Period:** None. **Eviction Process:** Former owners must be served with three day notice to quit property. New owner may then file eviction lawsuit. **Deficiency Judgments:** Allowed if brought in separate lawsuit within two years of sheriff sale. Amount of deficiency may be limited by fair market value of property. **Limits on Deficiency Judgments:** Action to pursue a deficiency must be brought into court within two years of auction date. If the borrowers ask the court to determine the fair market value, the deficiency may be limited or offset if the market value is greater than the price obtained at auction. **Cash Exempted in Bankruptcy:** $11,000 for single person, $22,000 for married couple. **State Statutes:** Tex. Prop. Code Ann. § 51.002.

Utah Foreclosure Laws

Expected Timeline: Four to five months **Security Instrument:** Mortgage or Deed of Trust. Deed of trust most common. **Type of Process:** Judicial or Non judicial. Non judicial most commonly used. **Protections for Service members:** Utah Code Ann. § 39-7-101 to 39-7-119 **Time to Respond:** Notice of default must be recorded at least three months before sale date. Notice must be mailed to homeowners within ten days of recording. Notice of sale must be published at least three times at least three months after notice of default is recorded. Last publication must be at least ten days before sheriff sale. Notice of sale must also be posted on property at least twenty days before auction date. **Reinstatement Period:** Homeowners may reinstate up to three months after notice of default is recorded. **Protections for High-Cost Mortgages:** None. **Redemption Period:** Redemption is allowed up to 180 days after sheriff sale date. **Eviction Process:** Former owners must receive a five day notice to quit property. New owner may then file eviction lawsuit. **Deficiency Judgments:** Allowed if brought in separate lawsuit after foreclosure auction. Amount is limited by fair market value of property. **Limits on Deficiency Judgments:** Action to pursue deficiency judgment must be made within three months of the sale date. Any judgment is limited to difference between the debt owed, including fees and charges on the account, and the fair market value. **Cash Exempted in Bankruptcy:** None. **State Statutes:** Utah Code Ann. § 57-1-19, 78-37-1, Utah R. Civ. Pr. 69(i),(j).

Vermont Foreclosure Laws

Expected Timeline: Seven to ten months **Security Instrument:** Mortgage or Deed of Trust. Mortgages most commonly used. **Type of Process:** Strict/judicial foreclosure if mortgage. Non judicial foreclosure if deed of trust. **Protections for Service members:** Vt. Stat. Ann. titl 12, § 553 **Time to Respond:** In judicial proceedings, homeowners have twenty to thirty days to answer foreclosure lawsuit. Under strict foreclosure, no sale takes place and title is transferred automatically to lender. In Non judicial proceedings, notice of intent to foreclosure must be served at least thirty days before notice of sale. Notice of sale must be served at least 60 days before sheriff sale date. **Reinstatement Period:** Homeowners may reinstate for at least thirty days after receiving notice of intent to foreclosure in Non judicial proceedings. **Protections for High-Cost Mortgages:** None. **Redemption Period:** In judicial proceedings, homeowners may redeem property for up to six months after sheriff sale. Judge may shorten redemption period. **Eviction Process:** In judicial proceedings, homeowners may redeem property for up to six months after sheriff sale. Judge may shorten redemption period. **Deficiency Judgments:** Allowed if requested in foreclosure lawsuit. Amount limited by fair market value if lender buys property back at sheriff sale. **Limits on Deficiency Judgments:** In judicial foreclosure proceedings, the lender must request deficiency in original complaint and will be limited to the fair market value if the mortgagee is the winner at auction. In strict foreclosure proceedings, a separate judgment must be obtained and is limited by the fair market value. **Cash Exempted in Bankruptcy:** $11,000 for single person, $22,000 for married couple. **State Statutes:** Vt. Stat. Ann. tit. 12, § 4526-4533, 4533a.

Virginia Foreclosure Laws

Expected Timeline: About two months **Security Instrument:** Mortgage or Deed of Trust. Deed of trust most commonly used. **Type of Process:** Judicial or Non judicial. Non judicial foreclosure most commonly used. **Protections for Service members:** Va. Code Ann. § 8.01-15.2 **Time to Respond:** Notice of sale must be served by mail or publication. Borrowers have 14 days to respond to service by mail. Notice by publication must be done for four consecutive weeks. Auction date may be eight to thirty days after last publication. **Reinstatement Period:** None. **Protections for High-Cost Mortgages:** None. **Redemption Period:** None. **Eviction Process:** Former owners do not need to be given notice before eviction lawsuit is filed. **Deficiency Judgments:** Allowed if brought in a separate lawsuit after sheriff sale. **Limits on Deficiency Judgments:** Deficiency judgments are allowed. **Cash Exempted in Bankruptcy:** $5,000 for single person, $10,000 for married couple. **State Statutes:** Va. Code Ann. § 55-59 to 55-66.6.

Washington Foreclosure Laws

Expected Timeline: Four to five months **Security Instrument:** Mortgage or Deed of Trust. Deed of trust most commonly used. **Type of Process:** Judicial or Non judicial. Non judicial most commonly used. **Protections for Service members:** Wash. Rev. Code § 4.16.220 **Time to Respond:** Notice of default must be served 30 days before notice of sale. Notice of default must be served by first class mail and registered/certified mail with return receipt requested. Notice must also be posted on the property or personal service. Notice of sale must be served in same manner as notice of default and must be done at least 90 days before sheriff sale. **Reinstatement Period:** Homeowners may reinstate the loan up to 11 days before sheriff sale. **Protections for High-Cost Mortgages:** None. **Redemption Period:** None. **Eviction Process:** New owner may file eviction lawsuit twenty days after foreclosure auction. **Deficiency Judgments:** Allowed in judicial foreclosures. Not allowed in Non judicial. **Limits on Deficiency Judgments:** Deficiency judgments are allowed in judicial foreclosure proceedings, but not if Non judicial foreclosure is pursued. **Cash Exempted in Bankruptcy:** $11,000 for single person, $22,000 for married couple. **State Statutes:** Wash Rev. Code § 61-24.020 to 61.24.140.

West Virginia Foreclosure Laws

Expected Timeline: About two months **Security Instrument:** Mortgage or Deed of Trust. Deed of trust most commonly used. **Type of Process:** Judicial or Non judicial. Non judicial most common. **Protections for Service members:** W. Va. Code § 11-21-61 **Time to Respond:** No specific time for notice is required under WV foreclosure law. Notice must be served within reasonable amount of time by publishing and sending through registered mail. **Reinstatement Period:** Homeowners may reinstate for ten days after being served with notice of right to cure. **Protections for High-Cost Mortgages:** W. Va. Code § 38-1-14 **Redemption Period:** None. **Eviction Process:** New owner will have to initiate lawsuit to get eviction order. This process may take two weeks to a month, depending on if former owners answer lawsuit or not. **Deficiency Judgments:** Allowed. **Limits on Deficiency Judgments:** Deficiency judgments are not allowed if the sales price is less than the amount of the indebtedness. **Cash Exempted in Bankruptcy:** $25,000 for single person and married couple. **State Statutes:** W. Va. Code § 38-1-3 to 38-1-15.

Wisconsin Foreclosure Laws

Expected Timeline: Up to ten months **Security Instrument:** Mortgage or Deed of Trust. Mortgage most common. **Type of Process:** Judicial or Non judicial. Judicial foreclosure most commonly used. **Protections for Service members:** Wis. Stat. § 21.75 **Time to Respond:** Homeowners have twenty to thirty days to respond to foreclosure lawsuit. Sheriff sale cannot be held until at least one year after judgment is entered in lawsuit. If lender waives right to deficiency judgment, auction may be held six months after judgment. **Reinstatement Period:** Homeowners may reinstate any time before final judgment in foreclosure case. Reinstatement may be possible after judgment if homeowners request it of the court. **Protections for High-Cost Mortgages:** None. **Redemption Period:** None. **Eviction Process:** Homeowners may keep possession of property until sheriff sale. **Deficiency Judgments:** Allowed if requested in initial foreclosure complaint. **Limits on Deficiency Judgments:** Deficiency judgments are allowed if included in the foreclosure action, but court must be satisfied that the house sold for its fair market value. If a lender waives its right to deficiency, the redemption period is shortened. **Cash Exempted in Bankruptcy:** $11,000 for single person, $22,000 for married couple. **State Statutes:** Wis. Stat. § 846.01 to 846.25.

Wyoming Foreclosure Laws

Expected Timeline: Two to three months **Security Instrument:** Mortgage or Deed of Trust. Deed of trust most commonly used. **Type of Process:** Judicial or Non judicial. Non judicial foreclosure most common. **Protections for Service members:** Wyo. Stat. Ann. § 19-11-101 to 19-11-124 **Time to Respond:** In judicial proceedings, homeowners have twenty to thirty days to respond to lawsuit. In Non judicial foreclosure, homeowners must be served with notice of intent to foreclose at least ten days before publication of notice of sale. Notice of sale is required to be published for four weeks before sale. Notice must also be served on homeowner before first publication. **Reinstatement Period:** None. **Protections for High-Cost Mortgages:** None. **Redemption Period:** Redemption period is three months after sheriff sale of property. **Eviction Process:** New owner will have to initiate eviction lawsuit in court after redemption expires. Process may take from two weeks to a month, depending on if former owners answer complaint or not. **Deficiency Judgments:** Allowed. **Limits on Deficiency Judgments:** Deficiency judgments are allowed if the homeowner is obligated by a separate written agreement. **Cash Exempted in Bankruptcy:** None. **State Statutes:** Wyo. State Ann. § 34-4-101 to 34-4-113, 1-18-101 to 1-18-114.

[Intentionally Blank]

ABOUT THE
CO–AUTHORS

Christopher J Crippen

Christopher has been in the real estate industry for the last 15 years. He started his career with a large national mortgage lender where
he managed a team of over 540 brokers
Prior to joining Cap Rate Residential, Christopher worked on the asset management side of the real estate business assisting Fannie Mae, First Republic and the FDIC with the disposition of their REO assets. While at the FDIC he led a team of 127 bank closing personnel,
asset managers, and support personnel in the closing of over
150 banks and disposition of over 25,000 REO assets.
Christopher is a lic'd Real Estate Professional,
Certified Distressed Property Expert, and a
Certified Investor Agent Specialist
He specializes in foreclosures, Bank REOs,
short sales, and residential investments
He teaches new and experienced investors how to Buy,
Rehabilitate, and re-sell distressed Real Estate.
"I know what it takes to get REO, Foreclosure, Short Sale and Investment deals DONE"
email crippen@REOTimes.com...
Sign up for the REO hot list: www.WholeSaleREOs.com

Tim & Julie Harris

Tim and Julie Harris have been leaders since day one of their careers. After selling more than 100 homes in their very first year and every year thereafter. They gained great acclaim when the National Association of Realtors named them Agents of the Year in 1997. They were consistently rated on the NARs lists of top 500 Agents in the US. They were also the youngest and fastest to achieve the Re/Max Platinum award. They are both Howard Brinton StarPower Stars, and have been long-time coaches for the Mike Ferry Organization. Having been involved in thousands of real estate transactions, Tim and Julie have shown their acumen not just for the business itself, but their abilities to impact their coaching clients.

Tim and Julie Harris are unique in the coaching and training field because they have actually done what they teach. In an industry filled with professional 'speakers' and 'gurus' whom have never sold real estate or haven't sold real estate in decades Tim and Julie stand out – Matter of fact, they are still involved in the real estate sales industry every day. Tim and Julie have contributed directly to the success of thousands of real estate professionals nationwide, through their unique and proven techniques. With over tens of thousands of coaching calls, they are proud to have some of the most successful agents in the country enrolled at The Harris Real Estate University. Every day, over 11,000 agents participate in a Harris Real Estate University coaching program.

For more information, find Tim and Julie Harris at:

www.HarrisRealEstateUniversity.com or **www.TimAndJulieHarris.com**.

www.ingramcontent.com/pod-product-compliance
Lightning Source LLC
Chambersburg PA
CBHW081404280526
45788CB00009B/2976